MATHS
NOW!
GET THE POINT!

3

MATHS NOW! 3

GET THE POINT!

GREEN ORBIT

**TONY &
MARY ELLEN BELL**

JOHN MURRAY

Other titles in this series:
Maths Now! Get the Point! Pupil's 1 0 7195 7276 2
Maths Now! Get the Point! Teacher's Resource File 1 0 7195 7277 0
Maths Now! Get the Point! Pupil's 2 0 7195 7278 9
Maths Now! Get the Point! Teacher's Resource File 2 0 7195 7279 7

Forthcoming:
Maths Now! Get the Point! Pupil's 4 0 7195 7354 8
Maths Now! Get the Point! Teacher's Resource File 4 0 7195 7355 6
Maths Now! Get the Point! Pupil's 5 0 7195 7356 4
Maths Now! Get the Point! Teacher's Resource File 5 0 7195 7357 2
Maths Now! Get the Point! Pupil's 6 0 7195 7358 0
Maths Now! Get the Point! Teacher's Resource File 6 0 7195 7440 4

© Tony and Mary Ellen Bell 1998

First published in 1998
by John Murray (Publishers) Ltd
50 Albemarle Street
London W1X 4BD

All rights reserved. No part of this publication may be reproduced in any material form (including photocopying or storing in any medium by electronic means and whether or not transiently or incidentally to some other use of this publication) without the written permission of the publishers, except in accordance with the provisions of the Copyright, Designs and Patents Act 1988 or under the terms of a licence issued by the Copyright Licensing Agency.

Layouts by Stephen Rowling/unQualified Design.
Artwork by Art Construction, Tom Cross, Mike Flanagan, Mike Humphries, Janek Matysiak.
Cover design by John Townson/Creation.

Typeset in 12/14pt Times by Wearset, Boldon, Tyne and Wear.
Printed and bound by G Canale, Torino, Italy.

A CIP catalogue record for this book is available from the British Library.

ISBN 0 7195 7352 1

Teacher's Resource File 3 ISBN 0 7195 7353 X

Contents

	Acknowledgements	vi
	How to use this book	1
UNIT 1	Number – Addition: up to 199	3
UNIT 2	Handling data – Block graphs, bar charts and pictograms	25
UNIT 3	Number – Place value to 2000	42
UNIT 4	Shape and space – Turns, angles and directions	60
UNIT 5	Number – Multiples of 3, 4 and 5	70
UNIT 6	Shape and space – 2D and 3D shapes	86
UNIT 7	Number – Decimal fractions	98
UNIT 8	Shape, space and measures – Estimating and measuring in mm, cm, m and km	116
UNIT 9	Number – Subtraction to 100	129
UNIT 10	Measures – Weight and capacity: g, kg, ml and l	151
UNIT 11	Number – Division by 2, 3, 4, 5 and 10	167
UNIT 12	Measures – Time: 24-hour clock and calendars	180

Acknowledgements

Cover reproduced by courtesy of John Dickinson/Tony Stone Images; **p.39**, **40**, **45** Last Resort Picture Library; **p.54** Rex Features; **p.72**, **73** Last Resort Picture Library; **p.76**, **77** John Townson/Creation; **p.87** *top* John Mead/Science Photo Library, *middle* John Townson/Creation; **p.101**, **106**, **131**, **144** Last Resort Picture Library; **p.152** John Townson/Creation; **p.153** Melvin Grey/NHPA; **p.161**, **164**, **171** Last Resort Picture Library.

The authors would like to thank Kim O'Driscoll, Researcher in low attainment in mathematics, University of Strathclyde, and all the schools and teachers throughout the country who helped in the development of this book.

How to use this book

This maths book is planned to help you understand and enjoy maths. You will be able to gain points which you will collect on a sheet so that you can see how well you are doing. You can swap these points for rewards.

In this book you will meet some symbols. They will tell you what you need and what to do. Here they are.

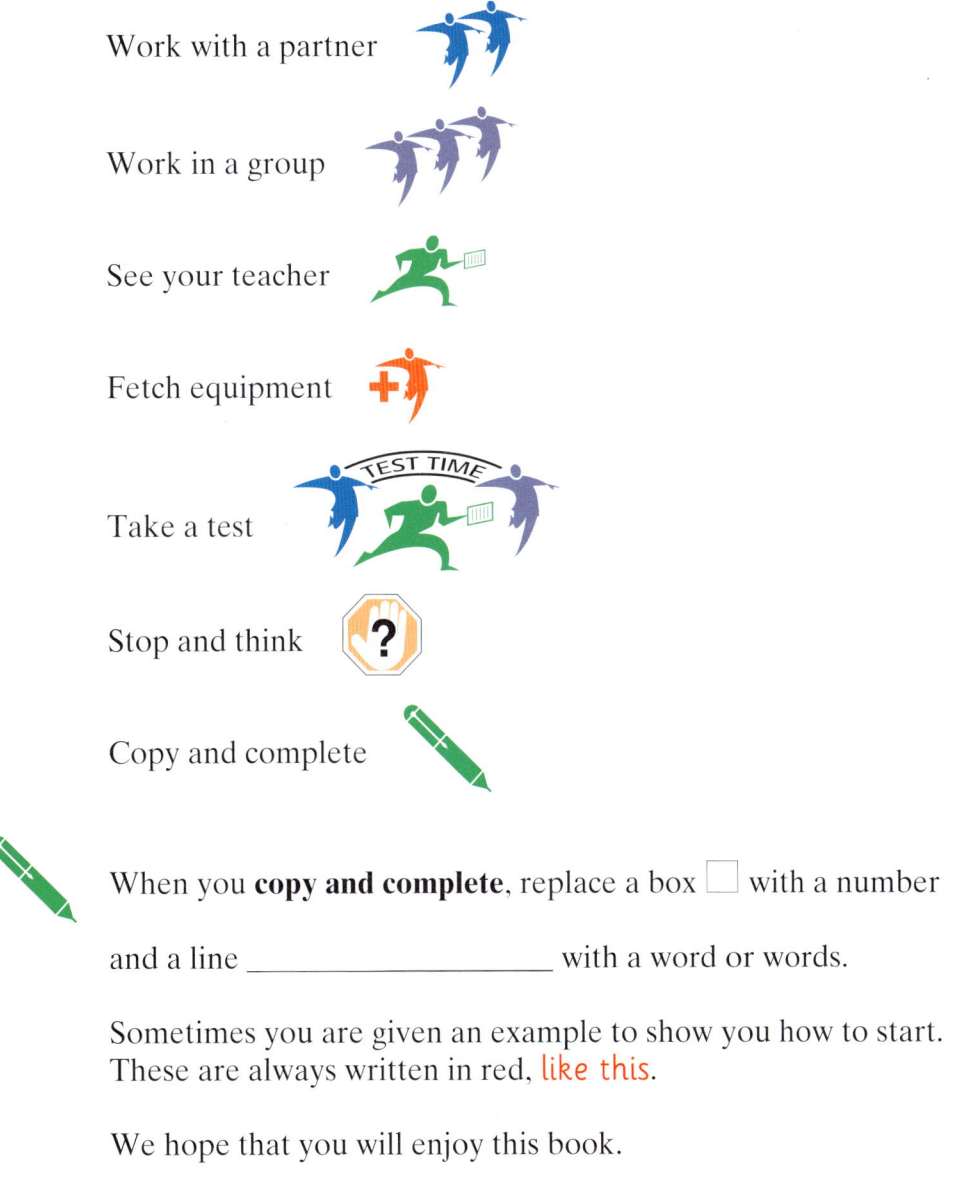

Work with a partner

Work in a group

See your teacher

Fetch equipment

Take a test

Stop and think

Copy and complete

When you **copy and complete**, replace a box ☐ with a number and a line _____ with a word or words.

Sometimes you are given an example to show you how to start. These are always written in red, like this.

We hope that you will enjoy this book.

1 Number

Addition: up to 199

Unit 1 words

more than	nearest	different
coins	group	roughly
single	digit	hour
plus	total	less than

Remember

Examples are shown in red.

 means copy and complete.

 You need
- a set of Unit 1 vocabulary Snap cards.

 Play a game of Snap to help you learn the words.

 Try the **word test** to get some points.

1 a) One 10p coin = **ten** 1p coins.

b) One 20p coin = _____ 1p coins.

c) One 50p coin = _____ 1p coins.

d) One £1 coin = _____ 1p coins.

4   UNIT 1 NUMBER

   2   You need
- coins.

a) 1p + 1p = ☐   b) 10p + 10p = ☐

c) 2p + 1p = ☐   d) 20p + 10p = ☐

e) 2p + 2p = ☐   f) 20p + 20p = ☐

g) 5p + 5p = ☐   h) 50p + 50p = ☐

i) 5 × 2p = ☐   j) 5 × 20p = ☐

k) 10 × 1p = ☐   l) 10 × 10p = ☐

3   Draw these bags.
Put an = sign between the pairs of bags which have the same amount of money.

a)

b)

c)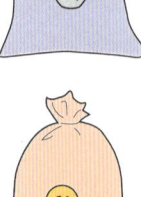

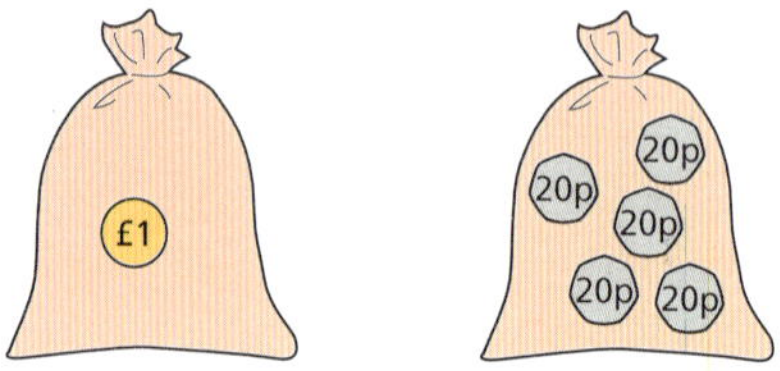

Addition: up to 199   5

d)

e)

f)

4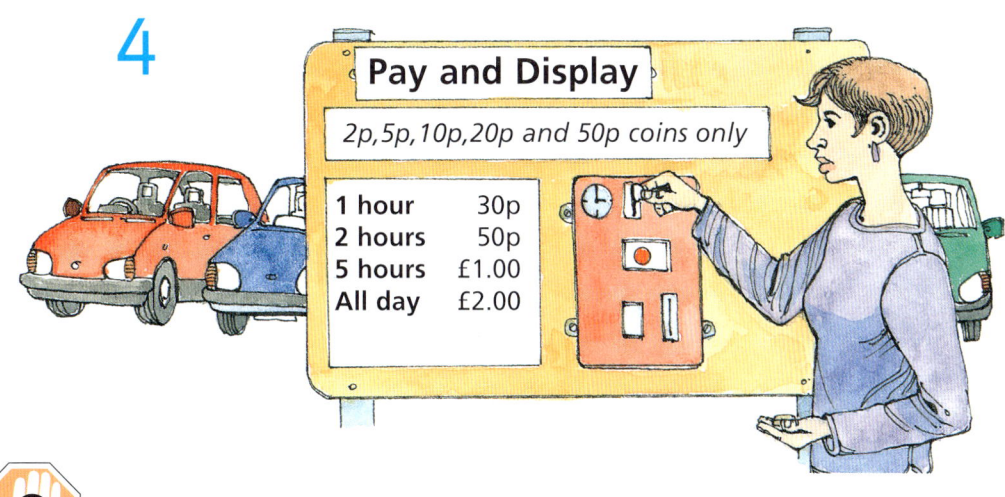

Pay and Display

2p, 5p, 10p, 20p and 50p coins only

1 hour	30p
2 hours	50p
5 hours	£1.00
All day	£2.00

a) Sue paid for one hour.
   She only had 10p coins.
   How many coins did she need?

b) Ben paid for two hours.
   How many different ways could he pay?

c) Lee paid for five hours. He has only 10p, 20p and 50p coins.
   How many different ways could he pay?

UNIT 1 NUMBER

 5 Try Worksheet 1 *Which hand?*

6 What is the value of the circled digit – **tens** or **units**?

a) ①5

a) **1 ten**

b) 8④   c) 9⓪   d) ②9

 7 a) 9 + 6 = [15]
[15] = [1] ten and [5] units

b) 9 + 9 = ☐
☐ = ☐ ten and ☐ units

c) 6 + 4 = ☐
☐ = ☐ ten and ☐ units

d) 8 + 5 = ☐
☐ = ☐ ten and ☐ units

e) 8 + 8 = ☐
☐ = ☐ ten and ☐ units

 8 Try Worksheet 2 *Change the money.*

Addition: up to 199 7

 9 You need
- coins.

Remember

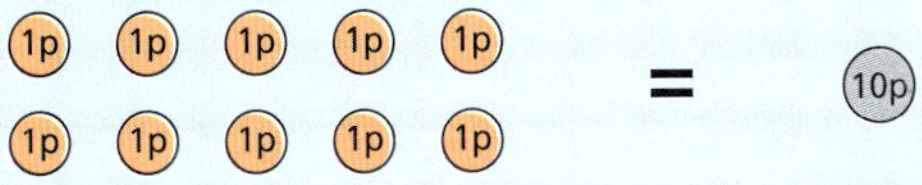

a) 11p + 9p = 20p

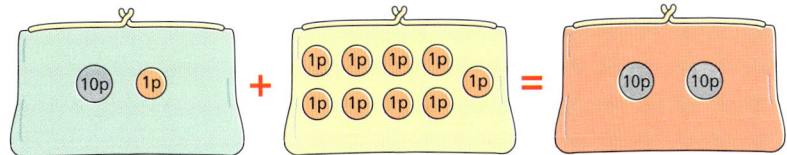

b) 9p + 12p = ☐   c) 9p + 13p = ☐

d) 14p + 9p = ☐   e) 8p + 15p = ☐

f) 16p + 7p = ☐   g) 8p + 17p = ☐

h) 14p + 8p = ☐   i) 16p + 6p = ☐

 10 You need
- base 10 blocks.

 Use base 10 blocks to show how you added and grouped to do these sums.

 Explain to a partner how you did the sum.

a) 13 + 9 = ☐   b) 19 + 6 = ☐

c) 17 + 8 = ☐   d) 14 + 6 = ☐

UNIT 1 NUMBER

 11 You need
- base 10 blocks.

Look at the drawings. Write the sums.
Use the base 10 blocks to help you with the sums.

> **Remember**
> 10 **units** = 1 group of **ten**.

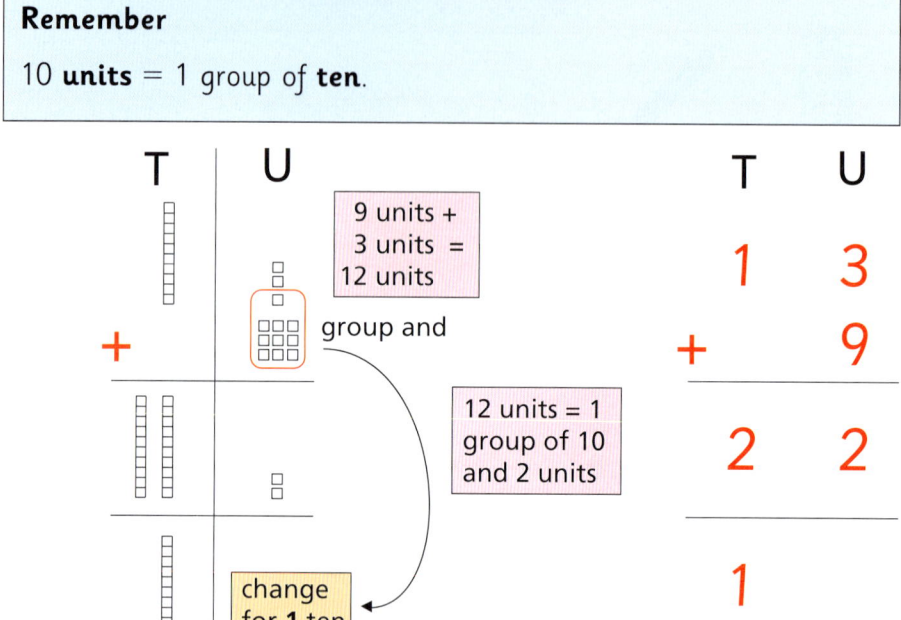

a) b) c)

Addition: up to 199   9

12 Look at the drawings to help you do the sums.

> **Remember**
> 10 single biscuits = 1 packet of 10.

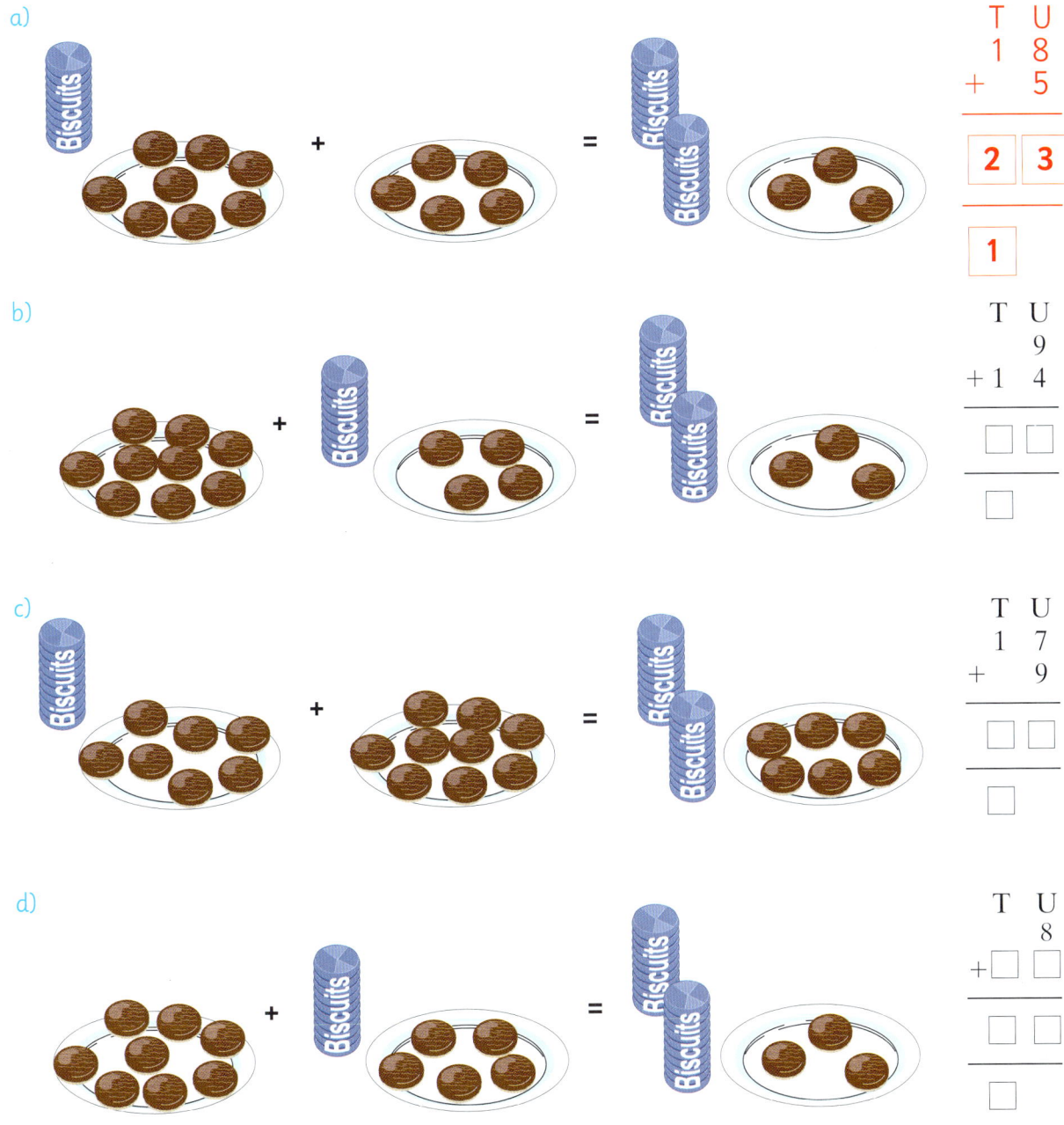

 **13** Try Worksheet 3 *Add and change*.

 **14** Copy the number lines or use Worksheet 4 to help you. Draw the arrows and complete the sums.

10 11 12 13 14 15 16 17 18 19 20 21 22 23 24 25 26 27 28 29 30

a) 16 + 4 = ☐

10 11 12 13 14 15 16 17 18 19 20 21 22 23 24 25 26 27 28 29 30

b) eighteen **and** five = ☐

10 11 12 13 14 15 16 17 18 19 20 21 22 23 24 25 26 27 28 29 30

c) 7 **plus** nineteen = ☐

 **15** a) 14 + 9 = 10 + **4** + **9**

= 10 + **13**

= **23**

b) 18 + 3 = 10 + ☐ + ☐

= 10 + ☐

= ☐

c) 16 + 7 = 10 + ☐ + ☐

= 10 + ☐

= ☐

d) 18 + 5

e) 16 + 8

f) 11 + 9

g) 13 + 9

h) 15 + 9

i) 16 + 4

Addition: up to 199   11

j) T U
    1 8
  +   6
   ☐☐
    ☐

k) T U
    1 4
  +   9
   ☐☐
    ☐

l) T U
    1 7
  +   7
   ☐☐
    ☐

m) T U
    1 3
  +   7
   ☐☐
    ☐

n) T U
    1 5
  +   5
   ☐☐
    ☐

o) T U
    1 4
  +   6
   ☐☐
    ☐

p) T U
    1 8
  +   8
   ☐☐
    ☐

q) T U
    1 9
  +   5
   ☐☐
    ☐

r) T U
    1 3
  +   9
   ☐☐
    ☐

s) T U
    1 9
  +   7
   ☐☐
    ☐

 16 You need

- base 10 blocks.

Use base 10 blocks to show how you added and grouped to do these sums.

a) 13 + 19 = ☐   b) 19 + 26 = ☐

c) 47 + 38 = ☐   d) 34 + 26 = ☐

 17 a) 20 is **2 tens** and **0 units**.

b) 50 is ☐ tens and ☐ units.

c) 90 is ☐ tens and ☐ units.

d) 30 is ☐ tens and ☐ units.

18 Write down the sums for these blocks of ten.

20 + 30 = 50

```
    T U
    2 0
The sum is  + 3 0
    ─────
    5 0
```

a)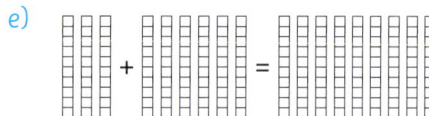

b)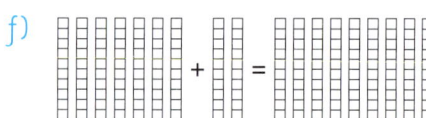

c)

d)

e)

f)

 **19** Copy the number lines or use Worksheet 4 to help you. Draw in the arrows and complete the sums.

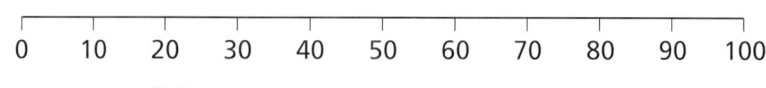

 a) 10 + 10 = ☐

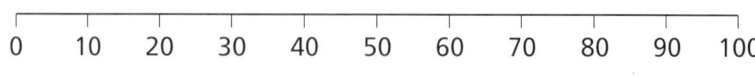

b) 50 **plus** twenty = ☐

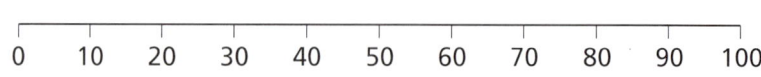

c) The **total** of fifty and forty = ☐

Addition: up to 199 • 13

 **20** a) 20 + 40 = ☐   b) 30 + 50 = ☐

c) 60 + 20 = ☐   d) 30 + 20 = ☐

e) 40 + 30 = ☐   f) 50 + 20 = ☐

g) 70 + 20 = ☐   h) 30 + 40 = ☐

i) 60 + 30 = ☐   j) 50 + 30 = ☐

k) 30 + 30 = ☐   l) 40 + 40 = ☐

 **21**

a) T U   b) T U   c) T U   d) T U
    2 0   4 0   6 0   3 0
  + 4 0   + 3 0   + 2 0   + 3 0
  ─────   ─────   ─────   ─────

e) T U   f) T U   g) T U   h) T U
    5 0   4 0   3 0   5 0
  + 4 0   + 4 0   + 6 0   + 3 0
  ─────   ─────   ─────   ─────

i) T U   j) T U
    2 0   1 0
  + 2 0   + 8 0
  ─────   ─────

14 UNIT 1 NUMBER

22 Look at the drawings to help you do the sums.

a)

```
  T U
  2 8
+ 1 5
  ___
  □ □
  ___
    □
```

b)

```
  T U
    9
+ 1 4
  ___
  □ □
  ___
    □
```

c)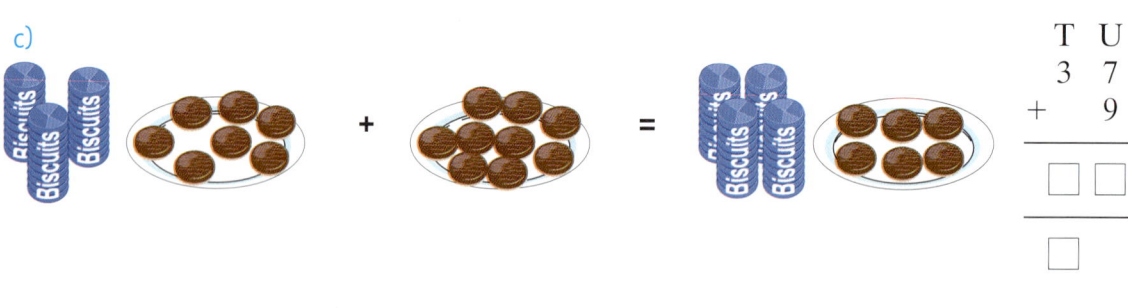

```
  T U
  3 7
+   9
  ___
  □ □
  ___
    □
```

d)

```
  T U
    8
+ □ □
  ___
  □ □
  ___
    □
```

 23 Try Worksheet 5 *Packet them*.

Addition: up to 199 15

24 a) 3 + 10 = 13　　b) 6 + 4 = 10　　c) 6 + 14 = 20
　　　13 + 10 = ☐　　　16 + 4 = ☐　　　16 + 14 = ☐
　　　23 + 10 = ☐　　　26 + 4 = ☐　　　26 + 14 = ☐
　　　33 + 10 = ☐　　　36 + 4 = ☐　　　36 + 14 = ☐
　　　43 + 10 = ☐　　　46 + 4 = ☐　　　46 + 14 = ☐
　　　53 + 10 = ☐　　　56 + 4 = ☐　　　56 + 14 = ☐
　　　63 + 10 = ☐　　　66 + 4 = ☐　　　66 + 14 = ☐
　　　73 + 10 = ☐　　　76 + 4 = ☐　　　76 + 14 = ☐

25　Try Worksheet 6 *Follow the pattern.*

26　What are the answers **roughly** – to the nearest ten?

a)　　1　6
　+　　　6
　─────
　　[2][2]　22 is **roughly** 20.
　─────
　　[1]

b)　1　8　　c)　2　7　　d)　3　6　　e)　2　5
　+　　9　　　+　　7　　　+　　5　　　+ 3　8
　─────　　　─────　　　─────　　　─────
　　☐☐　　　　☐☐　　　　☐☐　　　　☐☐
　─────　　　─────　　　─────　　　─────
　　☐　　　　　☐　　　　　☐　　　　　☐

f) 3 9
   +2 9
   □□
   □

g) 4 8
   +3 7
   □□
   □

h) 4 2
   +2 9
   □□
   □

i) 1 6
   +1 5
   □□
   □

j) 5 8
   +2 8
   □□
   □

k) 3 6
   +5 6
   □□
   □

l) 1 6
   +7 8
   □□
   □

27 Look at the drawings. Write the sums.

> **Remember**
>
> 10 groups of ten = 1 group of a hundred.

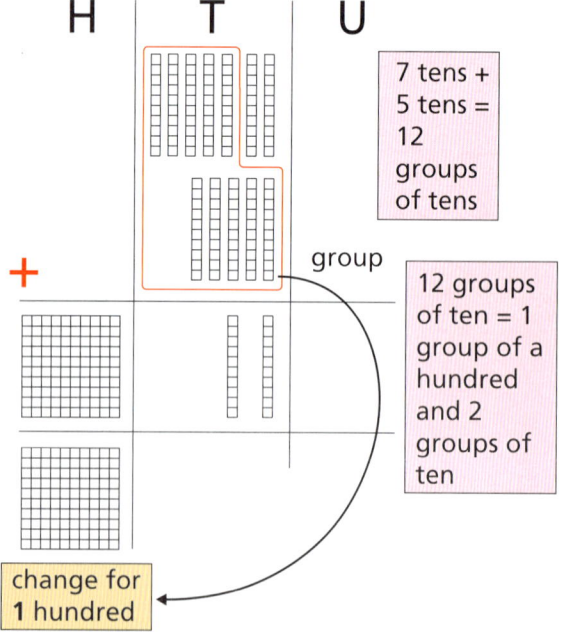

Addition: *up to 199* 17

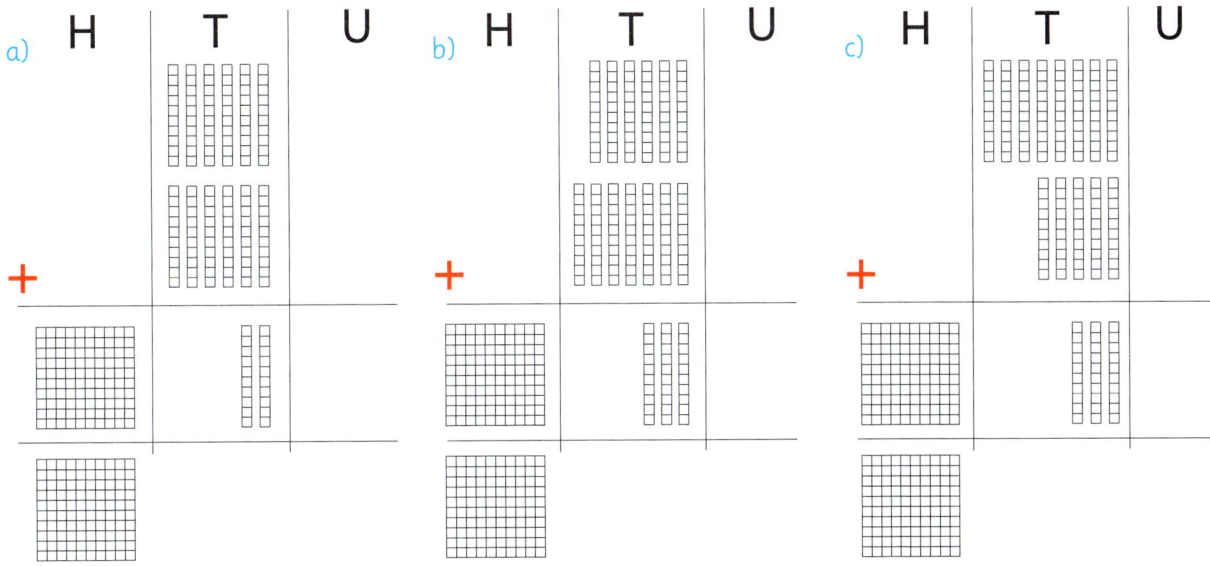

28 Try Worksheet 7 *Group the tens*.

29 Look at the drawings to help you do the sums.

> **Remember**
> Ten packets of 10 biscuits = 1 box of 100 biscuits.

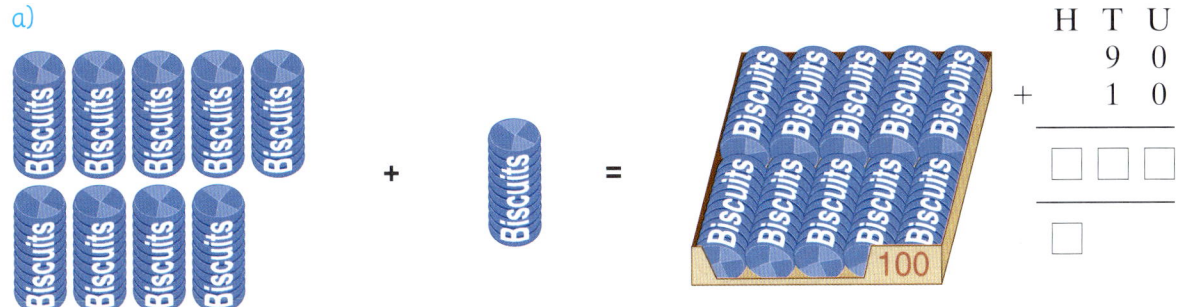

18 UNIT 1 NUMBER

b)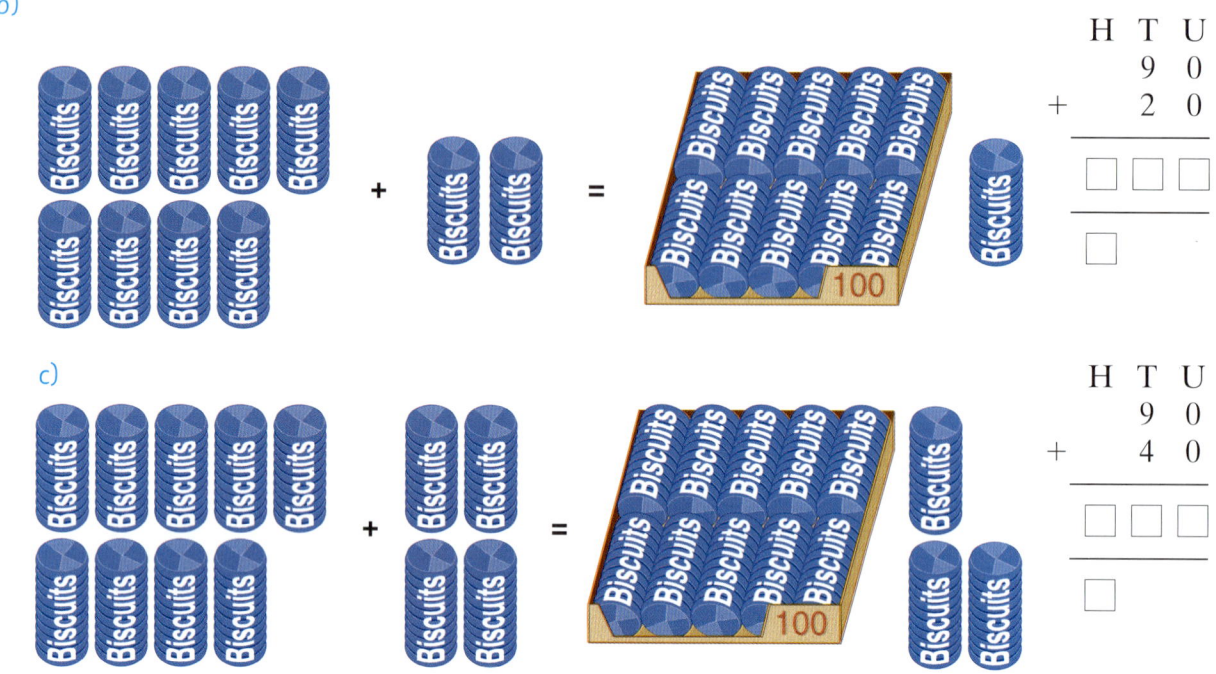

c)

30 Look at the drawings. Write the sums.

> **Remember**
> 10 groups of ten = 1 group of a hundred.

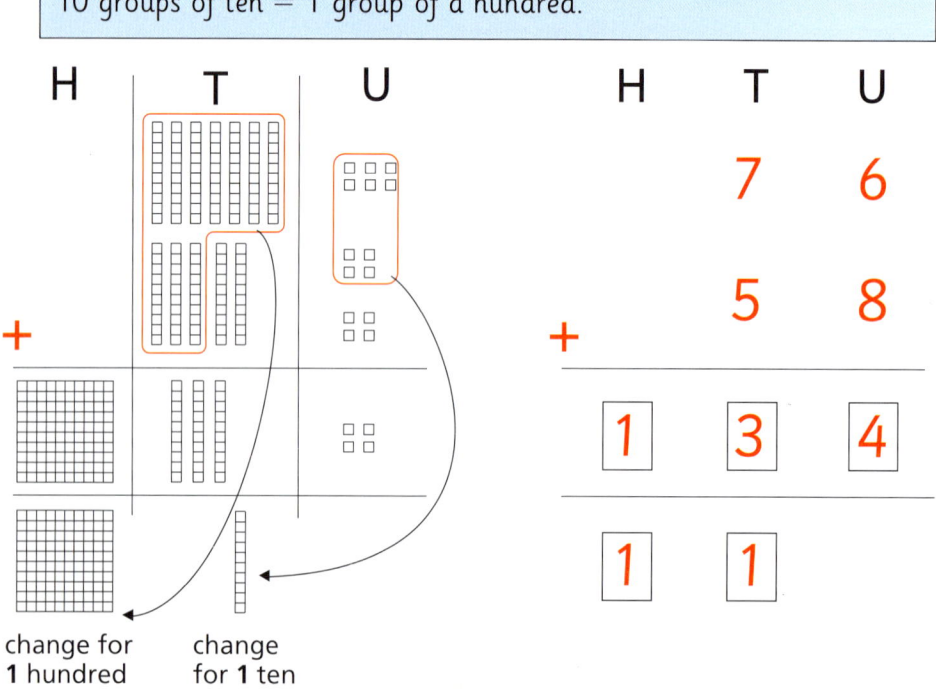

Addition: up to 199   19

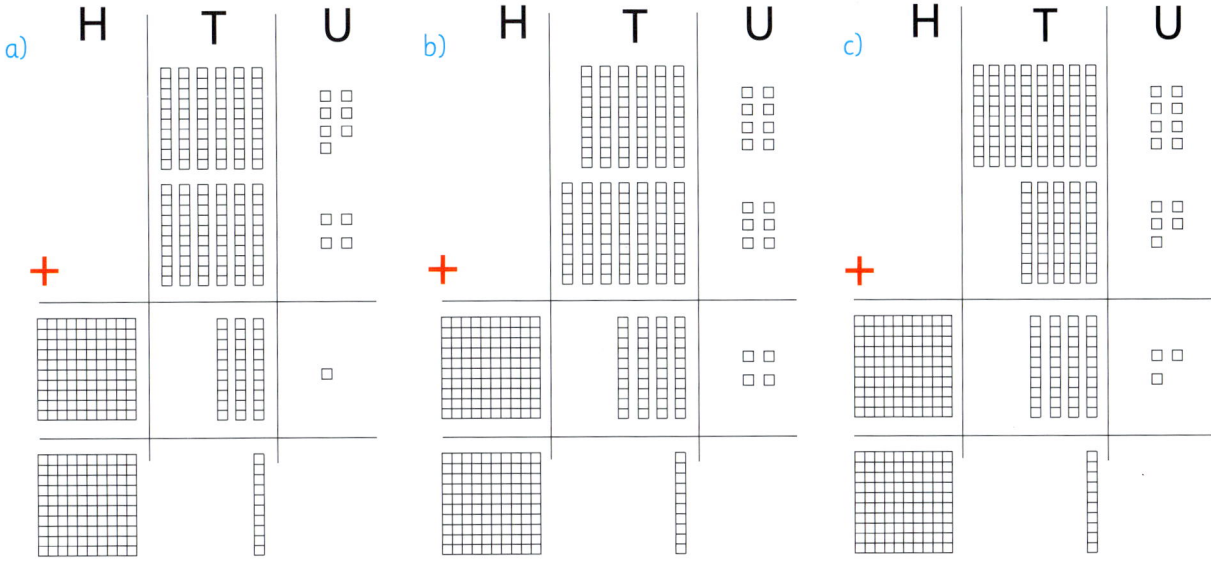

31

> **Remember**
>
> Check if you need to carry.

a) 8 6
  + 6 2
  ─────

b) 7 5
  + 6 5
  ─────

c) 4 4
  + 3 7
  ─────

d) 4 0
  + 6 0
  ─────

e) 5 3
  + 2 8
  ─────

f) 4 9
  + 3 9
  ─────

g) 7 8
  + 1 6
  ─────

h) 6 4
  + 3 3
  ─────

i) 6 5
  + 4 7
  ─────

j) 6 8
  + 5 8
  ─────

k) 7 5
  + 4 7
  ─────

l) 9 6
  + 2 5
  ─────

32 Lee chooses a meal.

Find out how much he would pay if he chose:

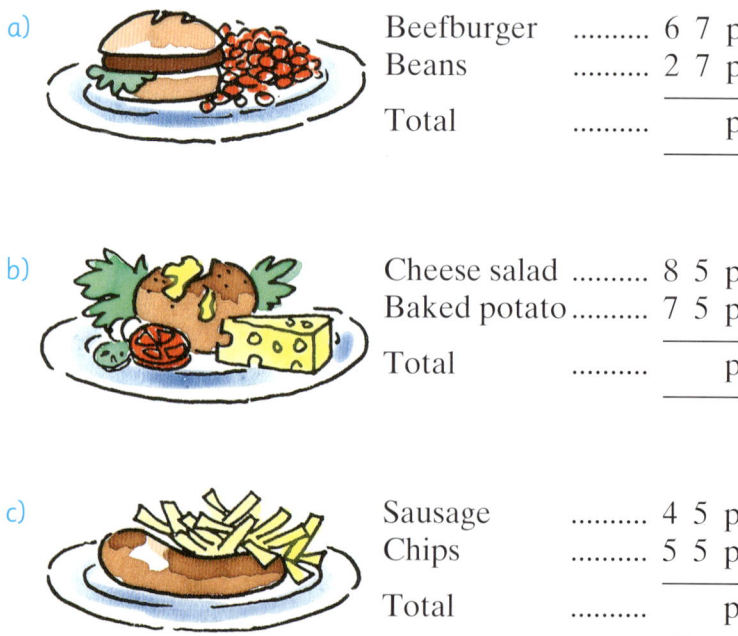

a) Beefburger .... 6 7 p
Beans .... 2 7 p
Total .... p

b) Cheese salad .... 8 5 p
Baked potato .... 7 5 p
Total .... p

c) Sausage .... 4 5 p
Chips .... 5 5 p
Total .... p

Addition: up to 199 • 21

d)

Biscuit	.... 1 9 p
Tea	.... 4 3 p
Total	.... ___ p

e) The **cheapest** meal was the _____

and the _____ .

The **dearest** meal was the _____

and the _____ .

f) List things on the menu which cost less than 50p.

g) Pick three meals which cost **more than** £1 (two items each meal).
What will the bill for each meal be?

 Try Worksheet Puzzle 10 *Check it out*.

 You need
- Unit 1 Race against time cards (1 set)
- your 'My maths record' sheet.

Race against time

1 Sort the race cards – this side up.

(8 + 8 = 16)
8 + 18

2 Take the cards one at a time.

3 Answer as quickly as you can.

4 Did you get it right?
Look at the other side of the card.

26

5 When you get all the answers correct, ask a friend to test you.

6 Now **Race against time**.

Go for points!

Ask your teacher to test and time you.

Remember

3 errors – 1 point

2 errors – 2 points

1 error – 3 points

0 errors – 5 points

Answer in 1 minute with 0 errors – 7 points

Now try Unit 1 Test.

Review 1

1 How many people does each column stand for?

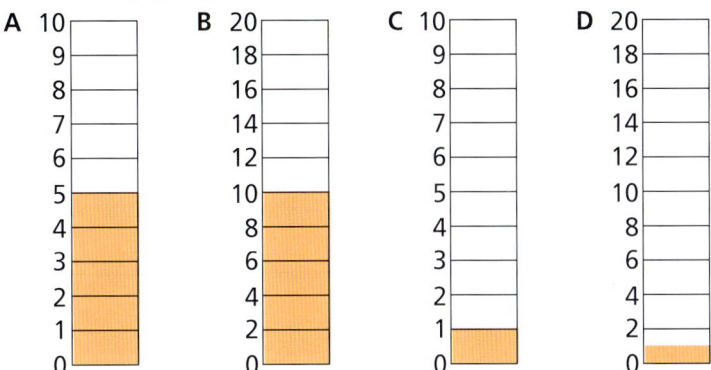

a) A = ☐ people   b) B = ☐ people

c) C = ☐ people   d) D = ☐ people

2  = 2 people

a)  = ☐ people   b)  = ☐ people

3 What are these numbers **roughly** – to the nearest **10**?

a) 41 is roughly ☐.   b) 48 is roughly ☐.

c) 45 is roughly ☐.   d) 141 is roughly ☐.

e) 148 is roughly ☐.   f) 145 is roughly ☐.

4

a) There are 6 people wearing shoes.
   How many shoes altogether?
   There are ☐ shoes altogether.

b) 7 people = ☐ shoes

c) 9 people = ☐ shoes

d) 3 people = ☐ shoes

e) There are 7 people with no shoes on.
   How many toes altogether?
   There are ☐ toes altogether.

f) 9 people = ☐ toes

g) 3 people = ☐ toes

5

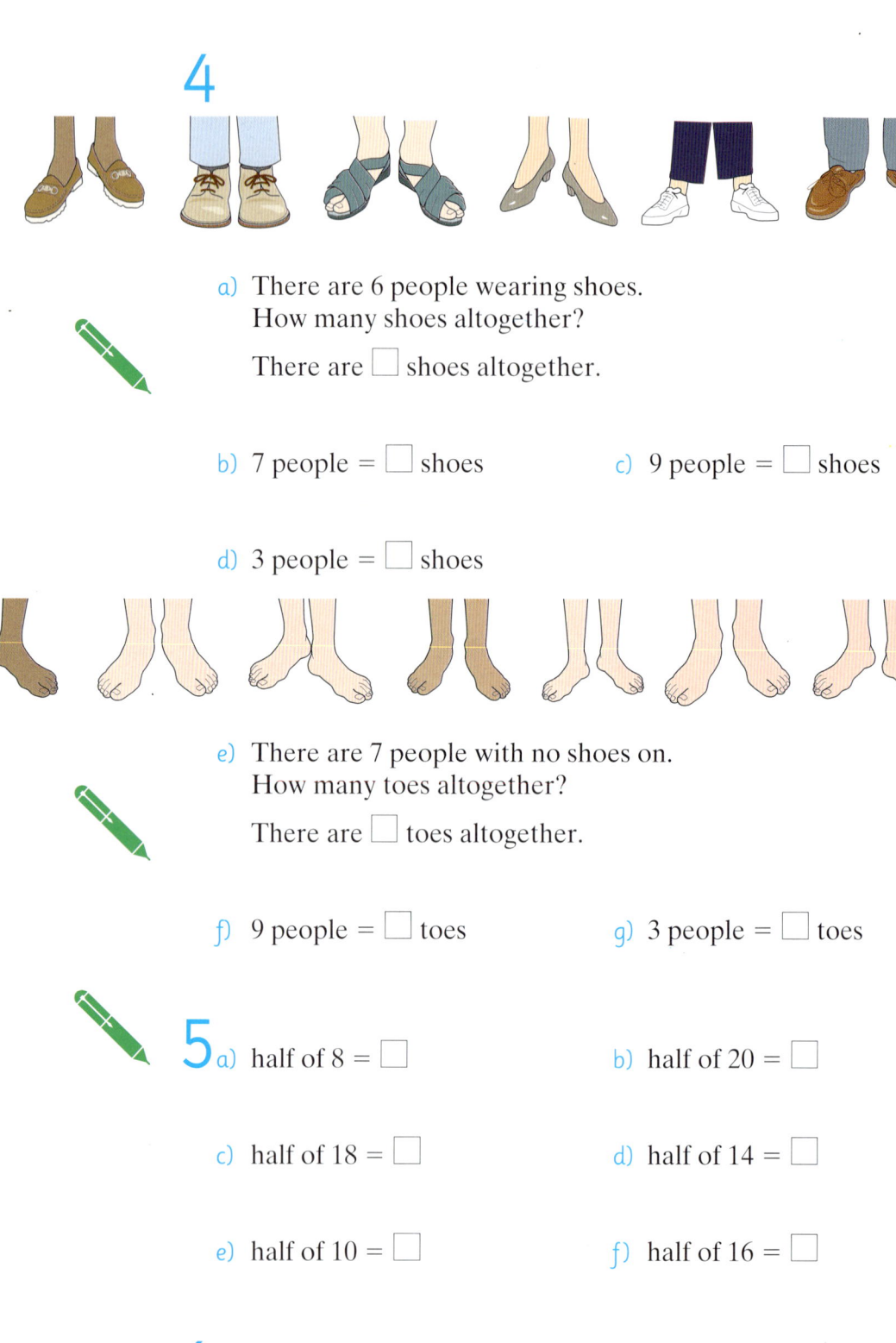

a) half of 8 = ☐

b) half of 20 = ☐

c) half of 18 = ☐

d) half of 14 = ☐

e) half of 10 = ☐

f) half of 16 = ☐

6 Write in order – **smallest** decimal number first.

0.5   0.1   0.9   0.7   1.0

2: Handling data

Block graphs, bar charts and pictograms

Unit 2 words

large	each	bar chart
pictogram	block graph	tally
divide	equal	hour
digit	single	plus

Remember

Examples are shown in red.

 means copy and complete.

 You need
- a set of Unit 2 vocabulary Snap cards.

 Play a game of Snap to help you learn the words.

 Try the **word test** to get some points.

UNIT 2 HANDLING DATA

1
How many people does each coloured **column** stand for?
Look carefully at each scale.

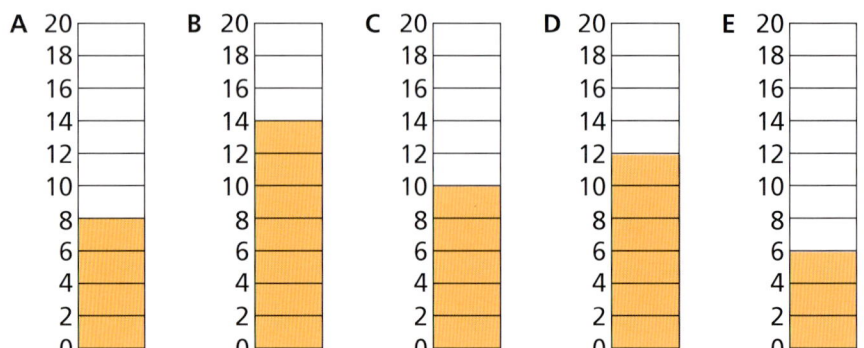

a) Column **A** shows **eight** people.

   Four blocks are coloured.

b) Column **B** shows _____ people.

   _____ blocks are coloured.

c) Column **C** shows _____ people.

   _____ blocks are coloured.

d) Column **D** shows _____ people.

   _____ blocks are coloured.

e) Column **E** shows _____ people.

   _____ blocks are coloured.

2
Fill in the missing numbers.

a) 2 ☐ 6 ☐ ☐ 12 ☐ 16 ☐ ☐

b) ☐ 4 ☐ 8 10 ☐ ☐ 16 ☐ 20

Block graphs, bar charts and pictograms   27

3 Here are the results of a **survey**. It is about the hours some people spend watching TV every day.

Number of hours	Number of people
less than 2 hours	IIII
2 hour	HHH III
3 hours	HHH HHH HHH III
4 hours	HHH HHH HHH I
5 hours	HHH HHH
more than 5 hours	HHH HHH II

You need

- squared paper or Worksheet 1.

Use the **tally table** to help you copy and complete the **block graph** below.

1 block 5 **2** people.

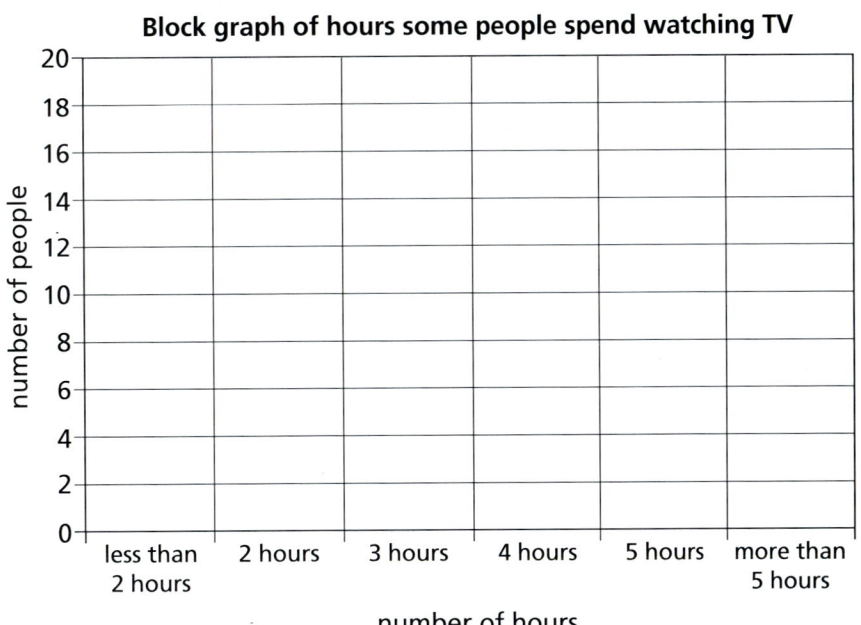

4 Look at the graph you have just drawn for **Question 3**.

a) ☐ people spend 2 hours watching TV.
☐ blocks have been coloured.

b) ☐ people spend less than 2 hours watching TV.
☐ blocks have been coloured.

c) ☐ people spend 4 hours watching TV.
☐ blocks have been coloured.

d) ☐ people spend 3 hours watching TV.
☐ blocks have been coloured.

e) ☐ people spend 5 hours watching TV.
☐ blocks have been coloured.

f) ☐ people spend more than 5 hours watching TV.
☐ blocks have been coloured.

g) What do you notice about each pair of answers?
What was the largest number of blocks coloured?
Why is this?

5 Use the tally table in **Question 3** to help you copy and complete the **pictogram** below.
Or you can use Worksheet 2 to help you.

Block graphs, bar charts and pictograms 29

Remember

Rules for drawing a pictogram

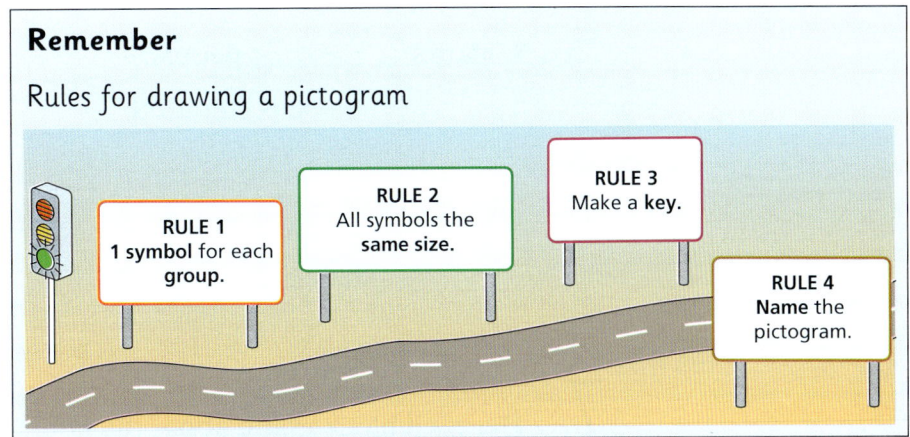

Pictogram of hours spent watching TV

Key: ♀ = 2 people

Number of hours	Number of people
less than 2 hours	
2 hours	
3 hours	
4 hours	
5 hours	
more than 5 hours	

6 How much of each is coloured?

A 0 2 4 6 8 10 12 14 16 18 20

B 0 2 4 6 8 10 12 14 16 18 20

C 0 2 4 6 8 10 12 14 16 18 20

D 0 2 4 6 8 10 12 14 16 18 20

a) **A** shows **six** people.

   Three blocks are coloured.

b) **B** shows _____ people.

   _____ blocks are coloured.

c) **C** shows _____ people.

_____ block is coloured.

d) **D** shows _____ people.

_____ blocks are coloured.

7 Here is a block graph about the hours a group of people spend watching TV.

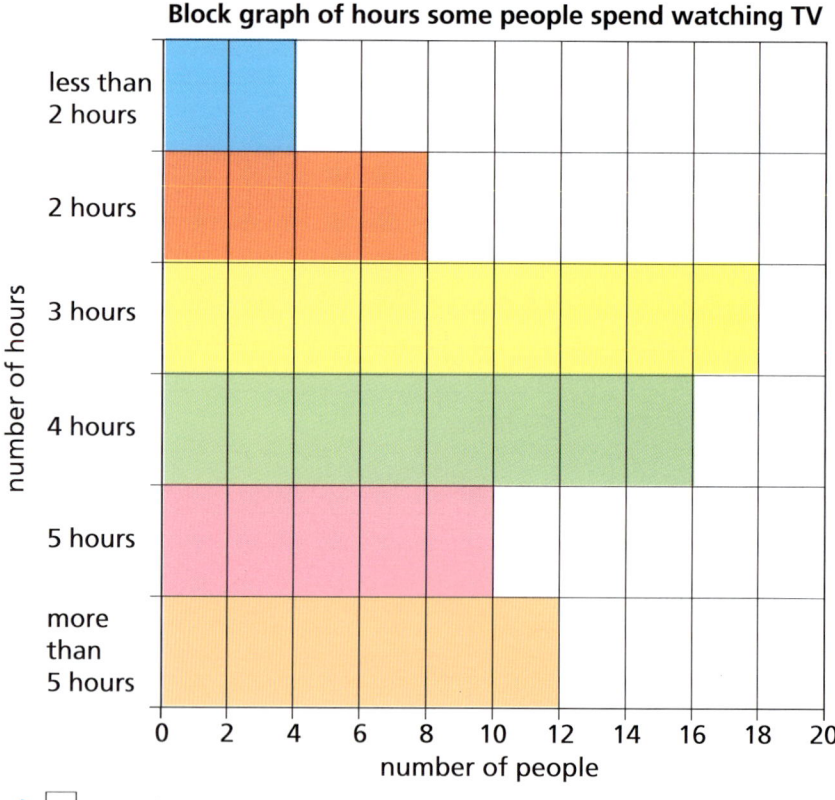

a) ☐ people spend 2 hours watching TV.

☐ blocks are coloured.

b) ☐ people spend less than 2 hours watching TV.

☐ blocks are coloured.

Block graphs, bar charts and pictograms • 31

c) ☐ people spend 4 hours watching TV.
☐ blocks are coloured.

d) ☐ people spend 3 hours watching TV.
☐ blocks are coloured.

e) ☐ people spend 5 hours watching TV.
☐ blocks are coloured.

f) ☐ people spend more than 5 hours watching TV.
☐ blocks are coloured.

g) What do you notice about the answers to **Question 7** and **Question 4**?

Why is this?

8 a) 10 ☐ 30 ☐ 50 ☐ 70 ☐ 90 ☐

b) ☐ 20 ☐ ☐ 50 ☐ ☐ 80 ☐ 100

c) Write these numbers in words.

20 **twenty**

50 _____   60 _____
80 _____   30 _____
70 _____   90 _____
40 _____

UNIT 2 HANDLING DATA

9 How many people does each coloured column stand for?

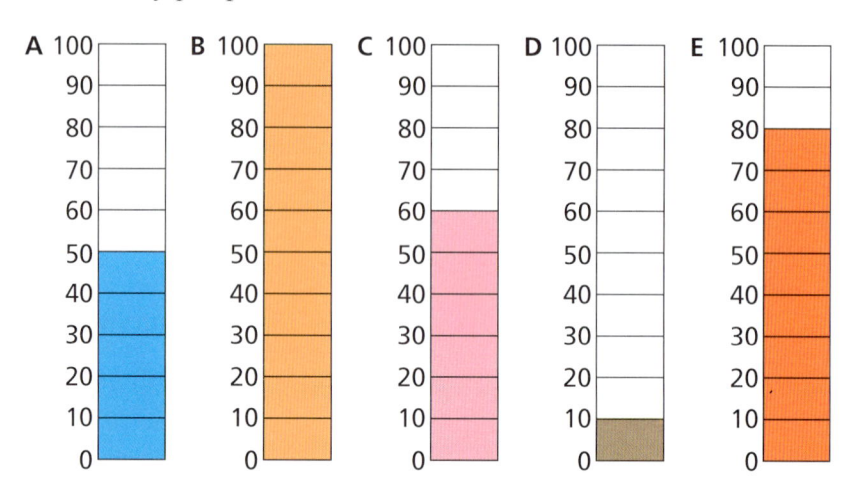

a) **A** shows ⬚50⬚ people.   ⬚5⬚ blocks are coloured.

b) **B** shows ⬚ people.   ⬚ blocks are coloured.

c) **C** shows ⬚ people.   ⬚ blocks are coloured.

d) **D** shows ⬚ people.   ⬚ blocks are coloured.

e) **E** shows ⬚ people.   ⬚ blocks are coloured.

10 Try Worksheet 3 *Colour the blocks (1)*.

Block graphs, bar charts and pictograms

11 Here are the results of a **survey** about the eye colours of a year group.

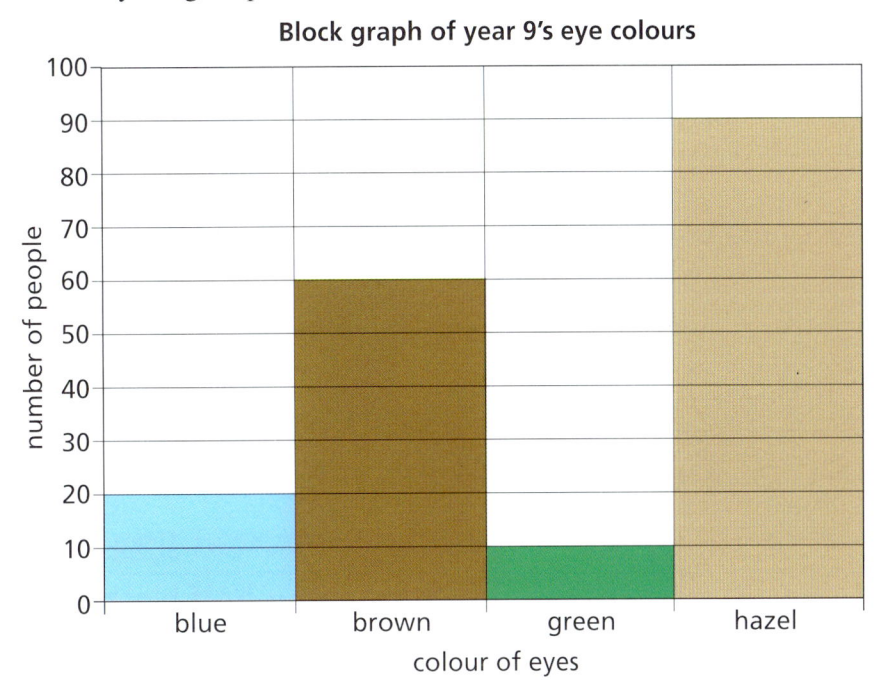

Block graph of year 9's eye colours

a) ☐ people had green eyes.

b) ☐ people had brown eyes.

c) ☐ people had blue eyes.

d) There were more _____ eyes than any other colour.

12 a) Half of 10 sweets = ☐ sweets.

b) 10 people divided by 2 = ☐ people.

c) 10 ÷ 2 = ☐

34 UNIT 2 HANDLING DATA

13 How many people does each coloured column stand for?

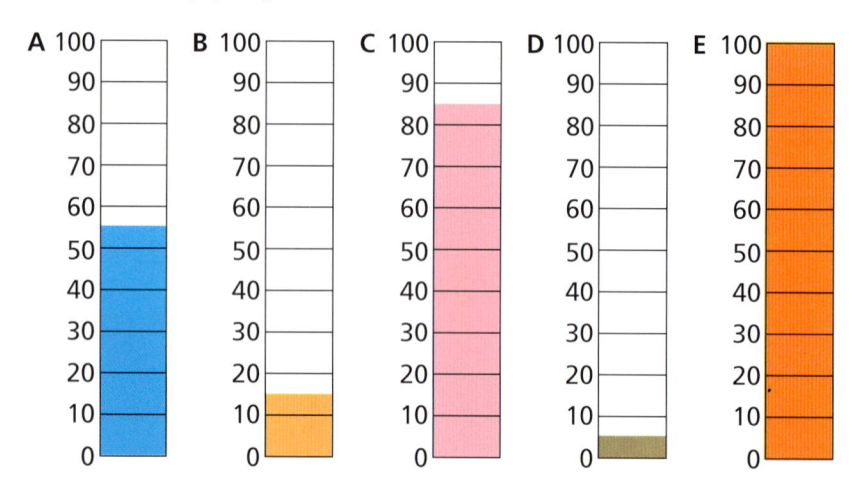

a) Column **A** shows **fifty-five** people.
   Five and a half blocks are coloured.

b) Column **B** shows _____ people.
   _____ blocks are coloured.

c) Column **C** shows _____ people.
   _____ blocks are coloured.

d) Column **D** shows _____ people.
   _____ blocks are coloured.

e) Column **E** shows _____ people.
   _____ blocks are coloured.

14 Try Worksheet 4 *Colour the blocks (2)*.

Block graphs, bar charts and pictograms 35

15

Remember
A **bar chart** is like a **block graph** with no lines.

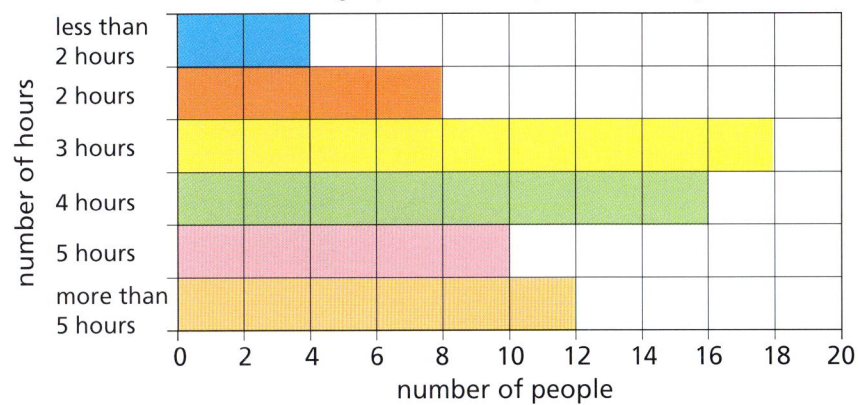

Block graph of hours spent watching TV

Bar chart of hours spent watching TV

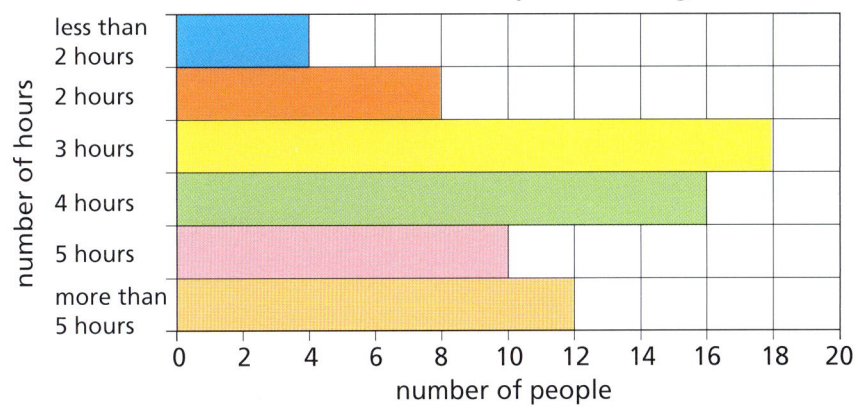

a) On the block graph, ☐ people watched TV for 2 hours.
   On the bar chart, ☐ people watched TV for 2 hours.

b) On the block graph, ☐ people watched TV for 5 hours.
   On the bar chart, ☐ people watched TV for 5 hours.

c) What do you notice about these answers?

16 Try Worksheet 5 *Colour the bars*.

UNIT 2 HANDLING DATA

17 Here is a **bar chart** about the eye colours of a group of people.

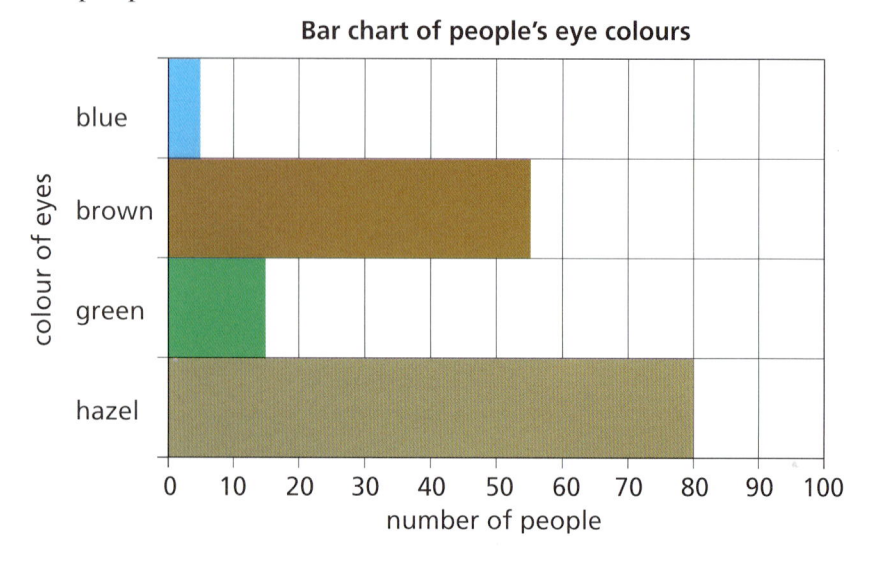

Bar chart of people's eye colours

(colour of eyes: blue, brown, green, hazel; number of people: blue ≈ 5, brown ≈ 55, green ≈ 15, hazel ≈ 80)

a) There were **more** people with _____ eyes than any other colour.

b) There were **fewer** people with _____ eyes than any other colour.

c) ☐ people had **either** blue or brown coloured eyes.

d) ☐ people had **either** green or hazel coloured eyes.

18 Try Worksheet 6 *Find the key*.

19 Show the information from the **bar chart** in **Question 17**, as a **pictogram**.

You can use Worksheet 7 to help you.

Use this **Key:** 👤 = 10 people

Block graphs, bar charts and pictograms   37

20   When we make a **guess** we can often use words on a scale from

certain ⟵ to ⟶ **impossible**

to describe how sure we are that something **will** or **will not** happen.

Write down **all the words you can think of** to say how likely it is that each of these things will happen.

The oceans will all dry up tomorrow.

I will own a car.

I will climb Everest.

I will watch TV tonight.

21   Try Worksheet 8 *Certain or not?*

UNIT 2 HANDLING DATA

22 Look at this bar chart.

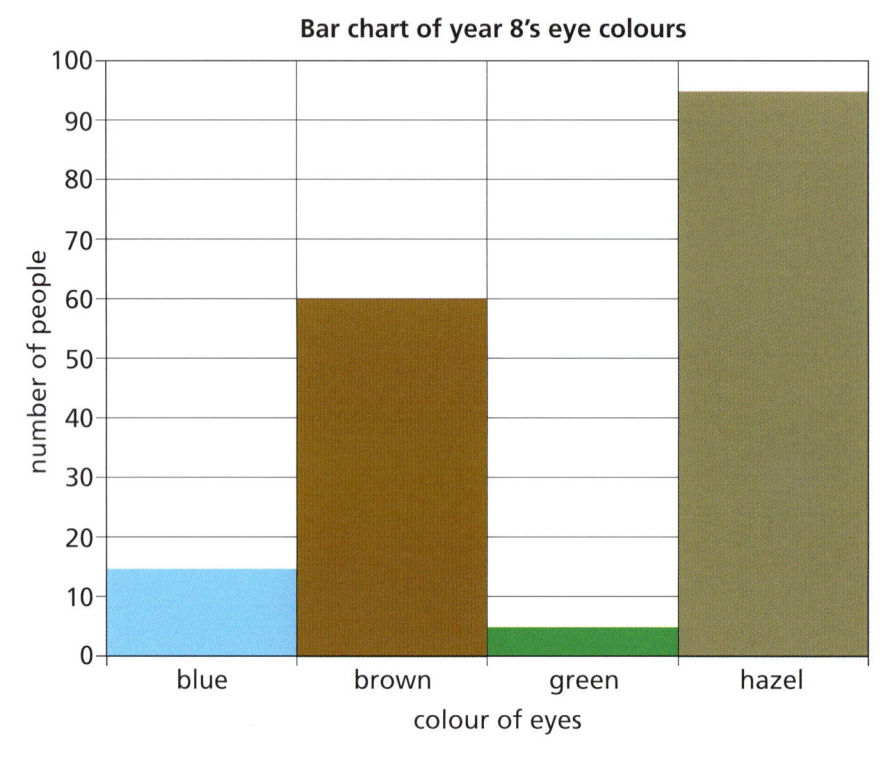

Bar chart of year 8's eye colours

(bar chart: blue ≈ 15, brown ≈ 60, green ≈ 5, hazel ≈ 95; y-axis: number of people; x-axis: colour of eyes)

Tracey is in year 8.
What colour are her eyes likely to be?
Match an eye colour to the words on the line.

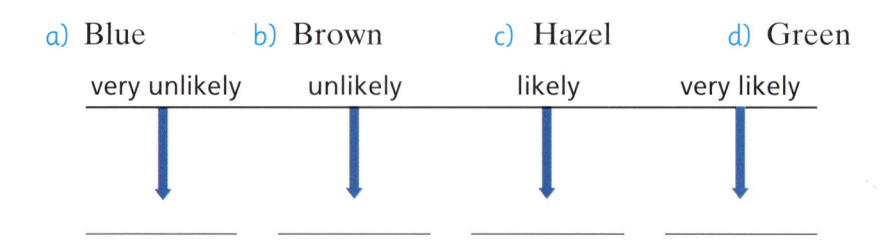

a) Blue   b) Brown   c) Hazel   d) Green

very unlikely   unlikely   likely   very likely

_____   _____   _____   _____

23 Try Worksheet Puzzle *Names*.

Now try Unit 2 Test.

Review 2

1 To help me remember, my:

a) **30 cm reminder** is _____ .

b) **1 m reminder** is _____ .

c) **1 kg reminder** is _____ .

d) **½ l reminder** is _____ .

2 Are these **measures** for **length** or measures for **weight**?

a) centimetres (cm) _____   b) grams (g) _____

c) metres (m) _____   d) kilograms (kg) _____

3 Are these **measuring tools** for **length** or measuring tools for **weight**?

a) _____

b) _____

UNIT 2 HANDLING DATA

c) _____

d) _____

e) _____

4 a) sixty = ☐ hundred, ☐ tens, ☐ units

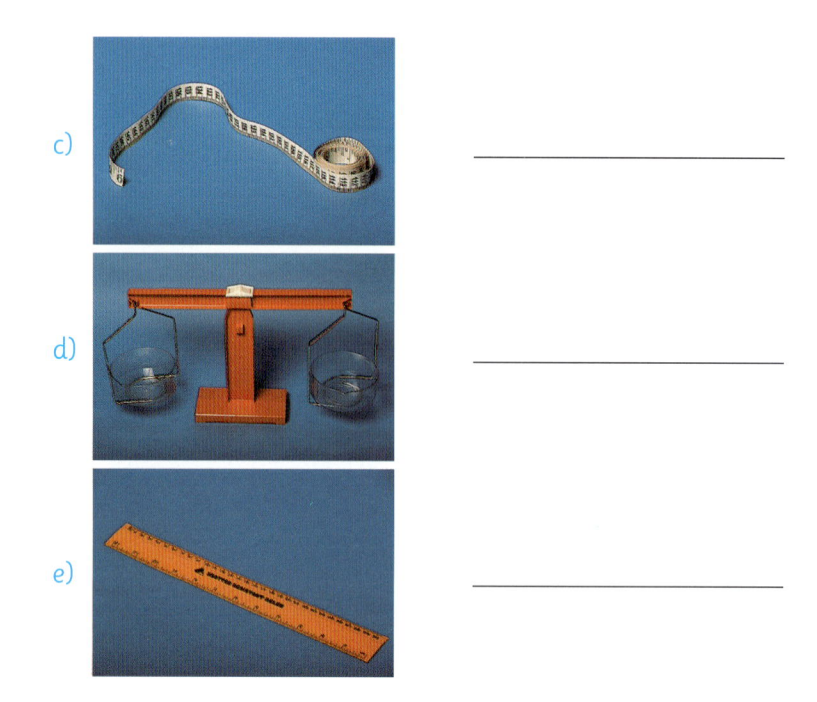

b) one hundred and six = ☐ hundred, ☐ tens, ☐ units

c) sixty-one = ☐ hundred, ☐ tens, ☐ units

5 Jade has £11. Sue has £6.

a) They have £☐ **altogether**.

b) The difference in their money is £☐.

c) Jade has £☐ more than Sue.

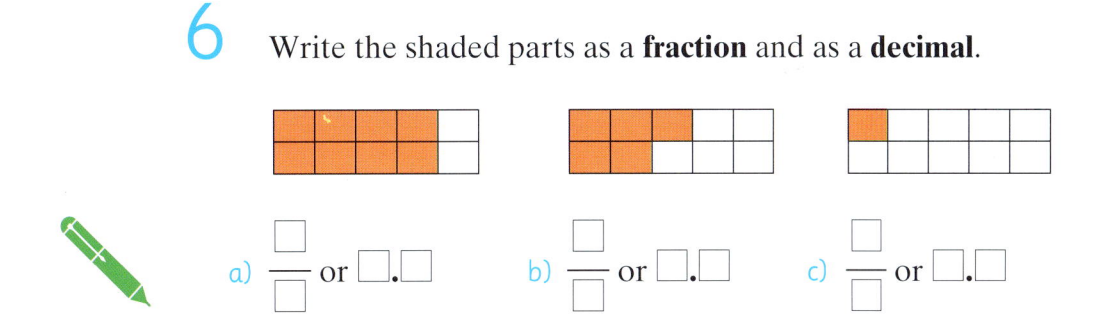

6 Write the shaded parts as a **fraction** and as a **decimal**.

a) $\dfrac{\square}{\square}$ or $\square.\square$

b) $\dfrac{\square}{\square}$ or $\square.\square$

c) $\dfrac{\square}{\square}$ or $\square.\square$

3 Number

Place value to 2000

Unit 3 words

thousand	same	worth
value	middle number	hundred
nearest	coins	group
large	roughly	single

Remember

Examples are shown in red.

means copy and complete.

You need
- a set of Unit 3 vocabulary Snap cards.

Play a game of Snap to help you learn the words.

Try the **word test** to get some points.

Place value to 2000 • 43

1 You may need
- a box of coins to help you.

Change these (1p) coins to the **smallest number** of coins.

Use (1p) (10p) and (£1) coins only.

Remember
Ten 1p coins = one 10p coin.
Ten 10p coins = one £1 coin.

a) Fifty 1p coins = **five** 10p coins and **no** 1p coins.

b) Twenty-six 1p coins = _____ 10p coins and _____ 1p coins.

c) Ninety-nine 1p coins = _____ 10p coins and _____ 1p coins.

d) One hundred 1p coins = _____ £1 coin, _____ 10p coins and _____ 1p coins.

e) One hundred and four 1p coins = _____ £1 coins, _____ 10p coins and _____ 1p coins.

f) One hundred and forty 1p coins = _____ £1 coins, _____ 10p coins and _____ 1p coins.

g) One hundred and twenty-six 1p coins = _____ £1 coins, _____ 10p coins and _____ 1p coins.

2 Which is worth most, a £1 coin or a 10p coin or a 1p coin?

a) A _____ coin is **worth most**.

b) A _____ coin has the **biggest value**.

Which is worth least, a £1 coin or a 10p coin or a 1p coin?

c) A _____ coin is **worth least**.

d) A _____ coin has the **least value**.

3 What is the value of the circled digits – **hundreds**, **tens** or **units**?

a) ⑦ 3 9: **7 hundreds**

b) 5 ⑧ 9   c) ⑨ 1 0   d) 8 6 ⑤

e) 9 ⑧ 4   f) 1 ⑦ 2   g) ⑦ 4 0

h) ③ 9 6   i) ⑨ 3 4   j) 9 ⓪

Place value to 2000 45

4 You need
- base 10 blocks.

Sue works in a shop at weekends.

She keeps some single biscuits on a plate for people to taste.

There are ten single biscuits in a packet.

There are ten packets in a box marked 100.

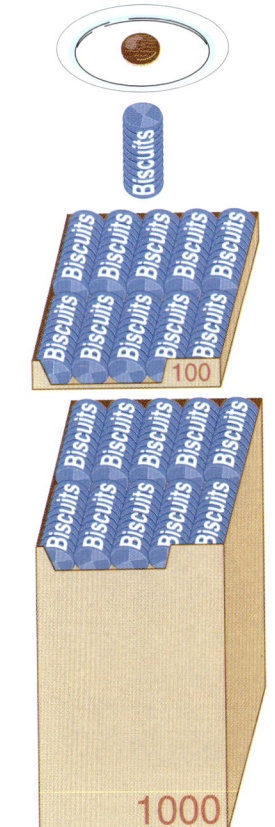

There are ten boxes of a hundred in a big box marked 1000.

46 UNIT 3 NUMBER

a) How many biscuits would there be if **a packet of ten** was added to the group below?

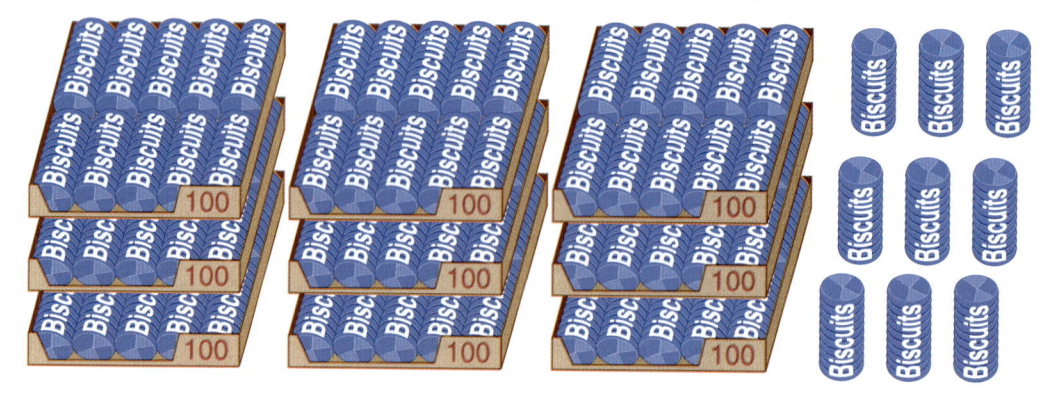

b) Draw the new group of biscuits.

c) 990 = ☐ hundred ☐ tens ☐ units.

d) 1000 = ☐ thousand ☐ hundreds ☐ tens ☐ units.

5 You need
- base 10 blocks.

a) How many biscuits would there be if **a single biscuit** was added to the group below?

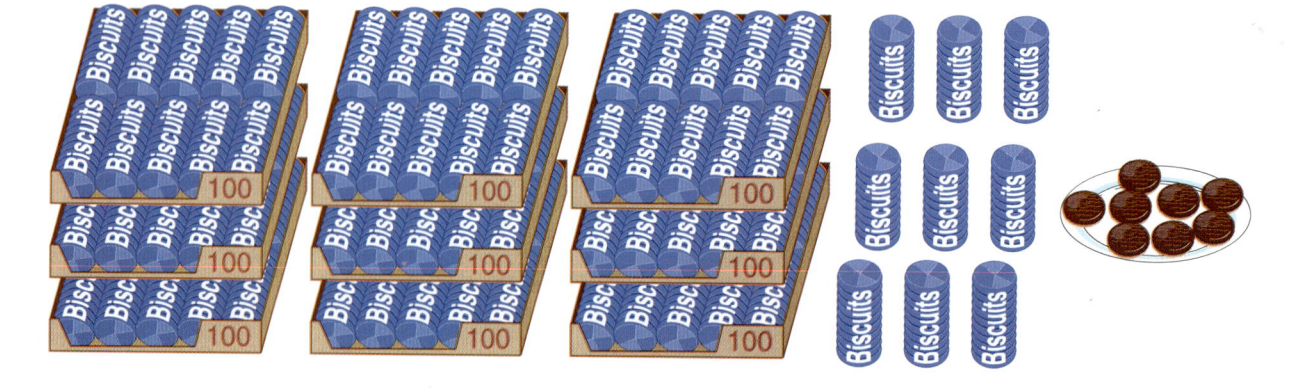

Place value to 2000 • 47

b) Draw the new group of biscuits.

c) 999 = ☐ hundreds ☐ tens ☐ units.

d) 1000 = ☐ thousand ☐ hundreds ☐ tens ☐ units.

6 How many biscuits are in each picture?

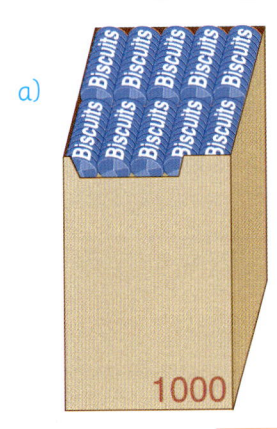

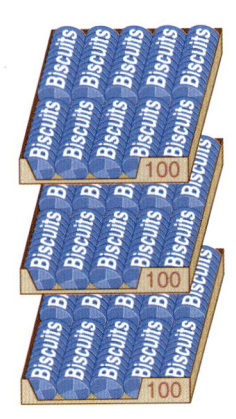

a) There are **1 3 2 4** biscuits.

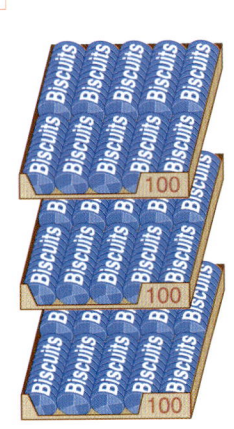

b) There are ☐ biscuits.

48 UNIT 3 NUMBER

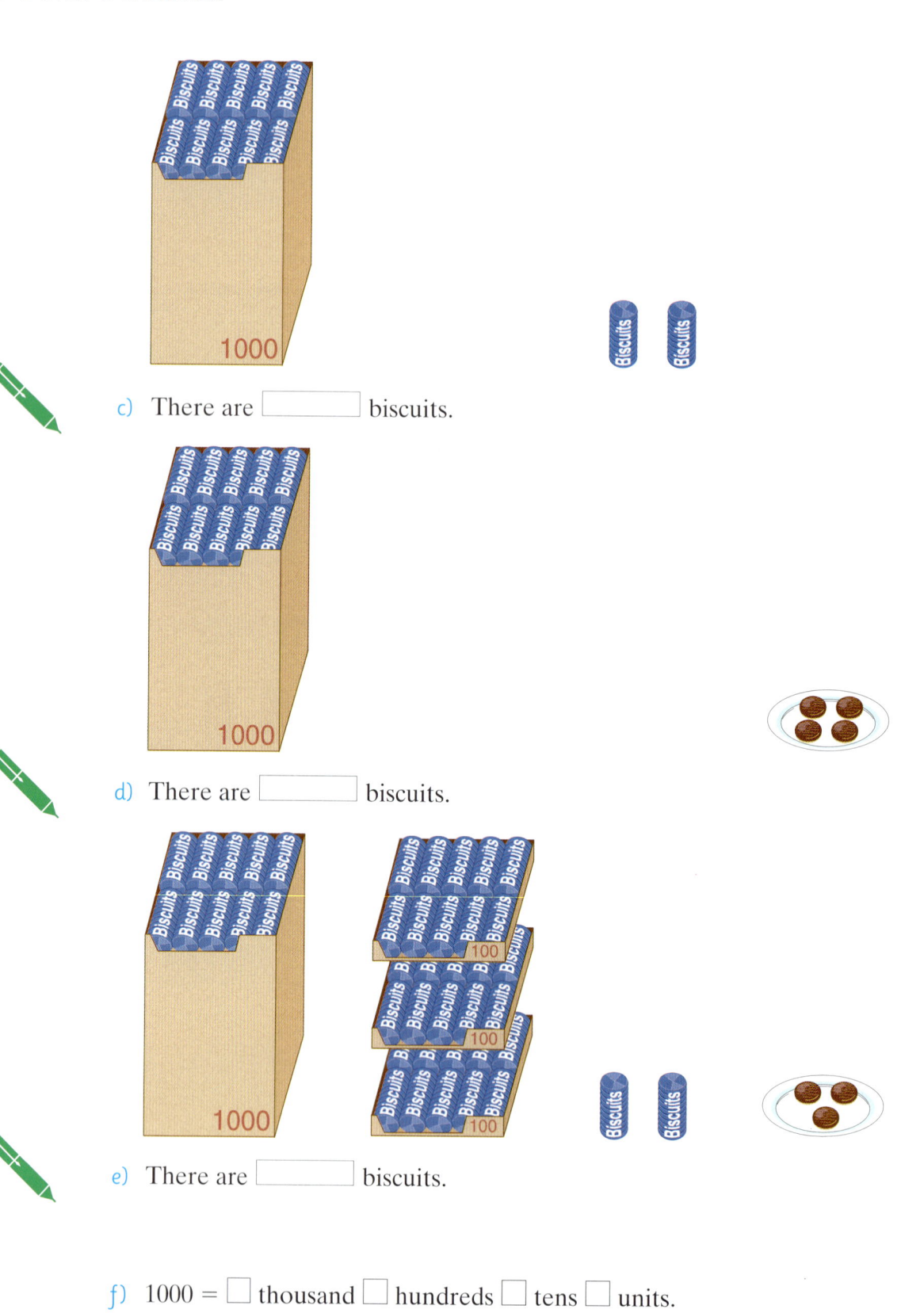

c) There are ☐ biscuits.

d) There are ☐ biscuits.

e) There are ☐ biscuits.

f) 1000 = ☐ thousand ☐ hundreds ☐ tens ☐ units.

Place value to 2000   49

g) 1400 = ☐ thousand ☐ hundreds ☐ tens ☐ units.

h) 1020 = ☐ thousand ☐ hundreds ☐ tens ☐ units.

i) 1003 = ☐ thousand ☐ hundreds ☐ tens ☐ units.

j) 1423 = ☐ thousand ☐ hundreds ☐ tens ☐ units.

7 You need
   • base 10 blocks.

Thousands   Hundreds   Tens   Units

a) There is ☐ thousand + ☐ hundred + ☐ ten + ☐ unit.
   There are ☐ altogether.

Thousands   Hundreds   Tens   Units

b) There is ☐ thousand + ☐ hundreds + ☐ ten + ☐ units.
   There are ☐ altogether.

50 UNIT 3 NUMBER

Thousands   Hundreds   Tens   Units

c) There is ☐ thousand + ☐ hundreds + ☐ ten + ☐ units.
There are ☐ altogether.

Thousands   Hundreds   Tens   Units

d) There is ☐ thousand + ☐ hundreds + ☐ tens + ☐ units.
There are ☐ altogether.

Thousands   Hundreds   Tens   Units

e) There is ☐ thousand + ☐ hundreds + ☐ tens + ☐ units.
There are ☐ altogether.

Place value to 2000 • 51

8 Find the **total**.

> **Remember**
> **Total** means **add**.

a) 500 + 40 + 3 = **543**

b) 600 + 20 = ☐

c) 700 + 3 = ☐

d) 300 + 30 + 9 = ☐

e) 800 + 2 = ☐

f) 200 + 1 + 9 = ☐

g) 1000 + 300 = ☐

h) 1000 + 30 = ☐

i) 1000 + 3 = ☐

9 Try Worksheet 1 *What value?*

10 How many **digits** are there in these numbers?

a) 3 = ☐ digit

b) 245 = ☐ digits

c) 1345 = ☐ digits

d) 48 = ☐ digits

e) The **smallest** number is ☐.

f) Write the numbers in order – **smallest** number first.

UNIT 3 NUMBER

11 Play a game of 'Speedy order'.

You need
- three dice.

a) Roll the dice to make a three-digit number.

b) You and your friend each write **four different numbers** using the same three digits each time.

c) Put the numbers you have made in order – **largest** number first.

d) The winner is the player who puts the four numbers in order faster.

> **Remember**
>
> To put numbers in order quickly, look at the **first** digit **5** 2 3.
>
> Try playing the same game with four dice to make four-digit numbers.

12 Try Worksheet 2 *Find the place*.

13 **Roughly** which number does the arrow point to each time?

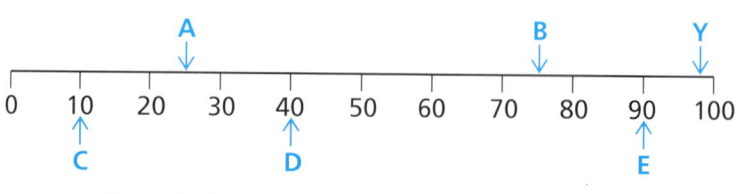

Arrow **A** = 25

Place value to 2000 • 53

14 What are these numbers **roughly** – to the **nearest ten**?

a) 29 is roughly 30.

a) 29 b) 129 c) 729 d) 529

e) 31 f) 131 g) 631 h) 731

i) 48 j) 448 k) 648 l) 948

m) 15 n) 215 o) 815 p) 115

15 Are these numbers nearer to 100 or nearer to 200? Use the number line below to help you.

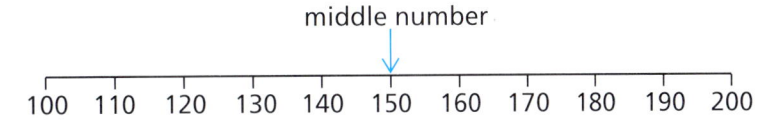

middle number ↓

100 110 120 130 140 150 160 170 180 190 200

a) 190 is nearer to _____ .

b) 180 is nearer to _____ .

c) 140 is nearer to _____ .

d) 120 is nearer to _____ .

e) 170 is nearer to _____ .

f) 110 is nearer to _____ .

54 UNIT 3 NUMBER

16 Lea wants to know how many people there are at the football match.

She does not want to know the **exact** number.
She wants to know **roughly**.

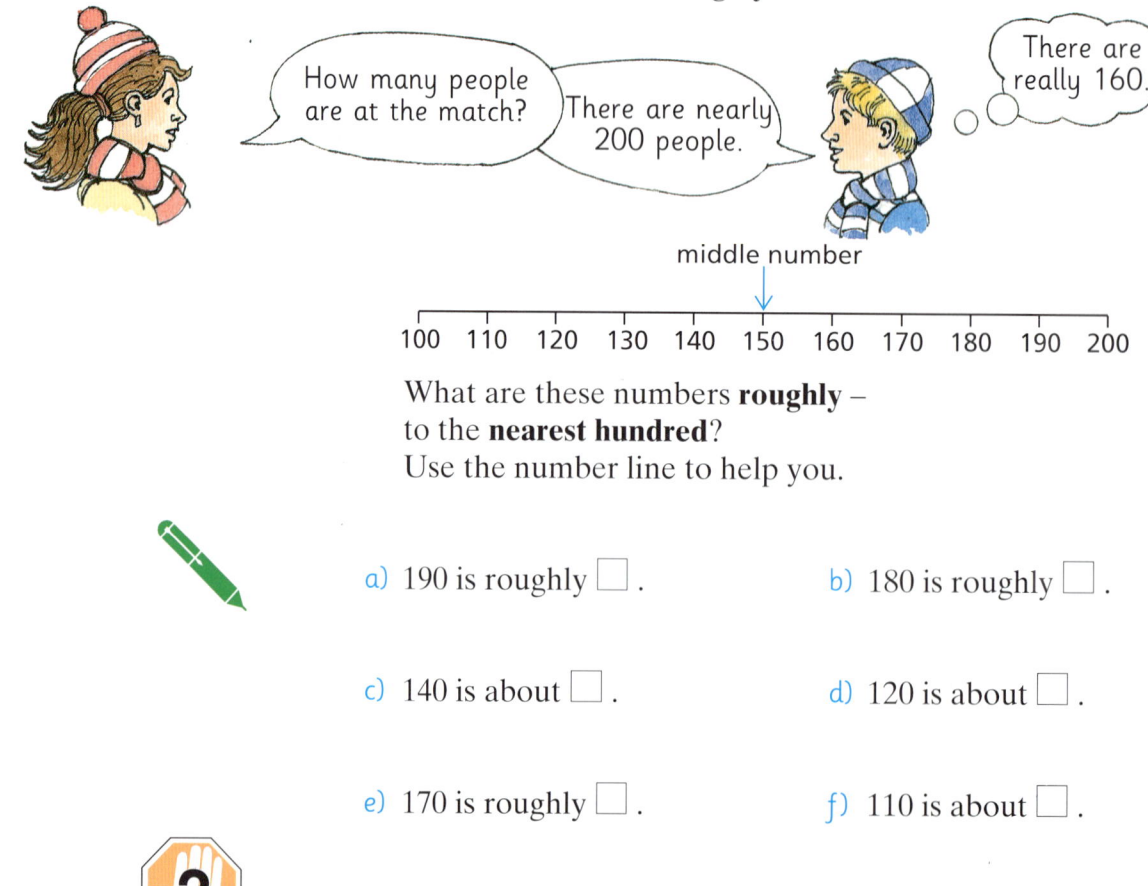

How many people are at the match?
There are nearly 200 people.
There are really 160.

middle number
↓
100 110 120 130 140 150 160 170 180 190 200

What are these numbers **roughly** –
to the **nearest hundred**?
Use the number line to help you.

a) 190 is roughly ☐.

b) 180 is roughly ☐.

c) 140 is about ☐.

d) 120 is about ☐.

e) 170 is roughly ☐.

f) 110 is about ☐.

g) What do you think 150 would be roughly?

Place value to 2000 • 55

17 What are these numbers **roughly** – to the **nearest hundred**?

a) 190   b) 350   c) 310   d) 140   e) 450

f) Write them in order – **smallest** number first.

18 Each arrow on the number line points to one of these numbers.

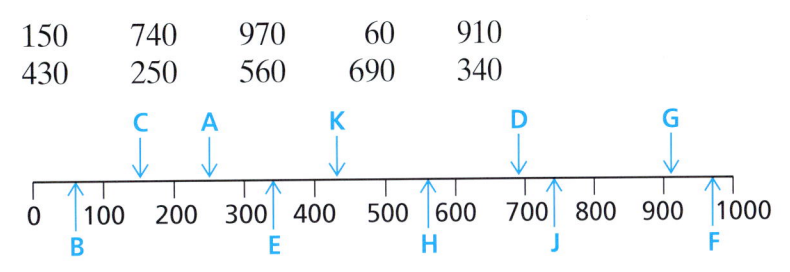

150   740   970   60   910
430   250   560   690   340

Match each arrow to the correct number.

Arrow **A** = 250

19 What are these numbers **roughly** – to the **nearest hundred**?

a) 192   b) 292   c) 127

d) 627   e) 225   f) 525

20 Write the numbers from **Question 19** – to the **nearest ten**.

UNIT 3 NUMBER

21 Try Worksheet 3 *On the line.*

22 You need
- a calculator.

Take turns to put these numbers into the calculator.

Take turns to guess the answers.

Look at the calculator to see if you are right.

a)	b)	c)
50 plus 10	1 + 100	99 + 1
500 plus 10	10 + 100	199 + 1
550 plus 10	100 + 100	590 + 10
800 plus 10	7 + 100	546 + 10
850 plus 10	70 + 100	834 + 100
900 plus 10	700 + 100	728 + 100
910 plus 10	650 + 100	890 + 100
980 plus 10	9 + 100	698 + 10
990 plus 10	90 + 100	10 + 1
1000 plus 10	900 + 100	99 + 10

23 You need
- Unit 3 Race against time cards (numbers and words)
- your 'My maths record' sheet.

Place value to 2000

Race against time

1 Sort the race cards – this side up.

⬜ ① 6 5 3

2 Take the cards one at a time.

3 Answer as quickly as you can:
'One thousand'.

4 Did you get it right?
Look at the other side of the card.

⬜ 1 thousand

5 When you get all the answers correct, ask a friend to test you.

6 Now **Race against time**.
Go for points!
Ask your teacher to test and time you.

> **Remember**
>
> 3 errors – 1 point
>
> 2 errors – 2 points
>
> 1 error – 3 points
>
> 0 errors – 5 points
>
> Answer in 1 minute with 0 errors – 7 points

Now try Unit 3 Test.

UNIT 3 NUMBER

Review 3

1 Would you use a **metre** or a **centimetre** measure to find the **length** of a table?

I would use a _____ measure.

2 Use a **centimetre ruler** to measure these lines.

a) ─────────────────────────────

b) ─────────────────────────

3 Write the times shown on these clock faces on the **digital** clocks.
Then write the time **in words**.

a) ☐ minutes past 1

b) ☐ minutes past 1

c) ☐ minutes past 1

d) ☐ minutes past 1

4 a) $8 \div 2 = \square$ b) $9 \div 2 = \square \, r \, \square$

c) $18 \div 2 = \square$ d) $19 \div 2 = \square \, r \, \square$

e) $60 \div 10$ f) $61 \div 10$

g) $64 \div 10$ h) $68 \div 10$

5 Which angle is a **right angle**? Angle A, B, C, or D?

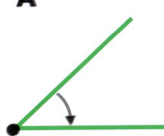

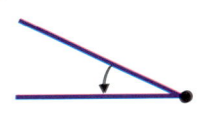

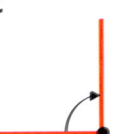

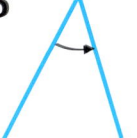

6 How many **right angles clockwise** or **anticlockwise** have these lines turned?

a)   b)

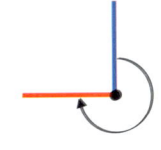

7 Which shapes are **symmetrical**?

hexagon   cuboid   quadrilateral   cylinder

4: Shape and space

Turns, angles and directions

Unit 4 words

direction	forward	North
South	East	West
turn	angle	clockwise
left	right	different

Remember

Examples are shown in red

✏ means copy and complete.

You need
- a set of Unit 4 vocabulary Snap cards.

Play a game of Snap to help you learn the words.

Try the **word test** to get some points.

Clockwise turns

Remember

Clockwise is the **same** way as a clock.
Anticlockwise is the **opposite** way to a clock.

Turns, angles and directions   61

clockwise – **same** as a clock

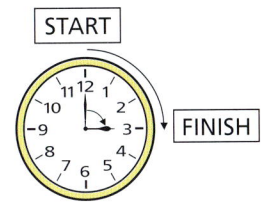

this hand has turned one **quarter** of a turn **clockwise**

anticlockwise – **opposite** to a clock

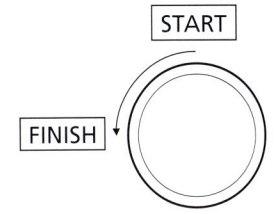

this screw top has turned one **quarter** of a turn **anticlockwise** to open

1 An arrow on the dial of a safe can move **clockwise** or **anticlockwise**.

The arrow on this safe **must go back to 0** after each turn. To get to 4 you could turn:

OR

a) Work out the moves to get to the numbers in the table below.

Remember

Always start at 0.

Number to get to	Clockwise	Anticlockwise
1		
2		
3		
4	4	8
5		
6		
7		
8		
9		
10		
11		

UNIT 4 SHAPE AND SPACE

b) Do you see a pattern? What is it?

c) The number which opens this safe is $\boxed{6\ 2\ 9}$.

To get this number you could turn:

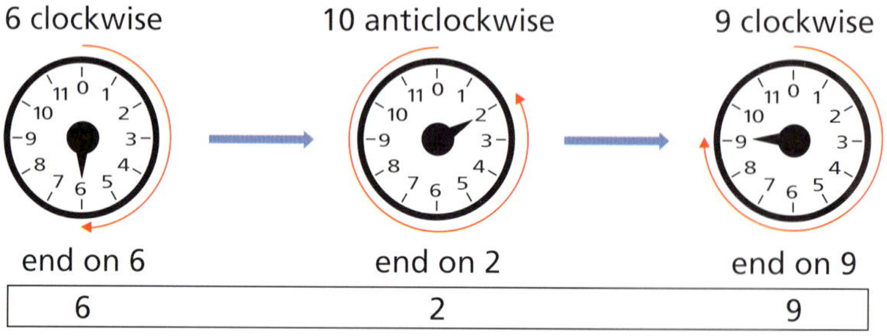

6 clockwise	10 anticlockwise	9 clockwise
end on 6	end on 2	end on 9
6	2	9

Can you think of other ways you could turn the arrow to get those digits?

2 The robber can't open your safe! Only you know that the number which opens your safe is $\boxed{9\ 1\ 8}$.

Which **two** of the groups of turns below will give $\boxed{9\ 1\ 8}$?

You can use a clock face with movable hand to help you.

Remember
The arrow moves back to zero after each turn.

a) 9 clockwise   11 anticlockwise   8 clockwise

b) 9 clockwise   8 anticlockwise   6 clockwise

c) 6 anticlockwise   11 anticlockwise   8 clockwise

d) 3 anticlockwise   1 clockwise   4 anticlockwise

Turns, angles and directions   63

3   If you go on a journey you may travel in different directions.
You can use a **code** to show directions from
START to FINISH.

> **FD F**orward   **RT**$\frac{1}{4}$ **R**ight **quarter** turn   **LT**$\frac{1}{4}$ **L**eft **quarter** turn

Look at the journey the arrows make across the tiles below.

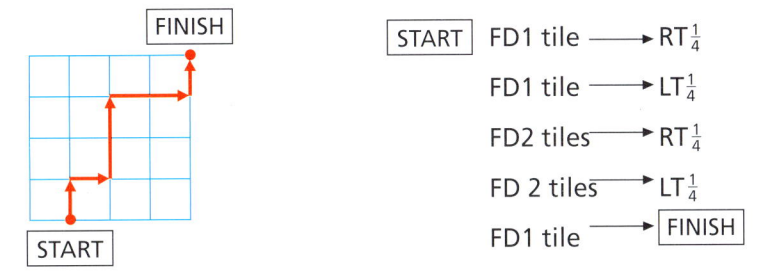

| START | FD1 tile ⟶ RT$\frac{1}{4}$ |
| FD1 tile ⟶ LT$\frac{1}{4}$ |
| FD2 tiles ⟶ RT$\frac{1}{4}$ |
| FD 2 tiles ⟶ LT$\frac{1}{4}$ |
| FD1 tile ⟶ FINISH |

Write out all the moves and turns to make the journey above.

START   forward 1 → right a quarter turn
forward 1 → left a quarter turn

4   You need

- squared paper.

a) Copy the journey below onto squared paper.

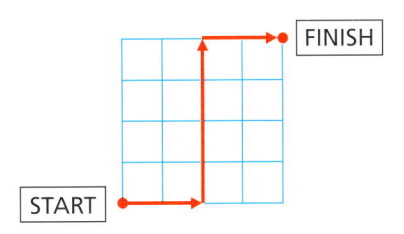

b) Write the moves and turns.
Use the codes **FD** and **RT**$\frac{1}{4}$ or **LT**$\frac{1}{4}$.
For each move, turn your book so that you are looking **up**
along the arrow each time.

UNIT 4 SHAPE AND SPACE

c) Tell your teacher how you think turning your book helps you.

5 Try Worksheets 1 and 2 *Journeys (1), (2)*.

6 You need
   - squared paper.

a) Find some **different** journeys to get from START to FINISH on these tiles.
Draw each one on squared paper.

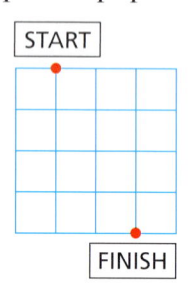

START

FINISH

b) Write the moves and turns for each journey using **FD** and **RT**$\frac{1}{4}$ or **LT**$\frac{1}{4}$.

7 When we go on journeys, we can find our way by following the direction of points around us – like these.

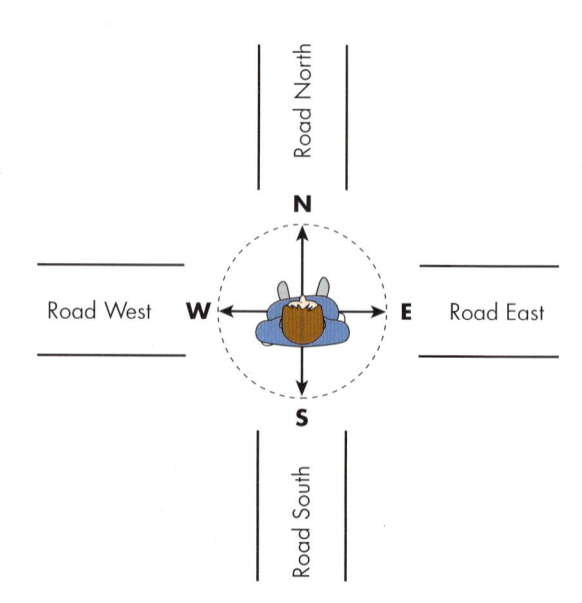

Road North

N

Road West W ← → E Road East

S

Road South

These are called **compass points**.

Turns, angles and directions • 65

N
W ← → E
S

these letters are short for ⇨

North
West ← → East
South

Copy the compass points into your book.

8 This church tower has a weather vane.

The cockerel's head **always** points to the direction the wind is coming **from**.

What direction is the wind coming **from** in each of these pictures?

a)

b)

c)

d)

UNIT 4 SHAPE AND SPACE

9 Can you think of a way to help you remember the missing **compass points**?

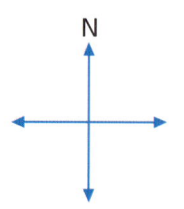

10 Try Worksheet 3 *Compass turns*.

11 Three cars go around town.
They cannot make a U-turn.

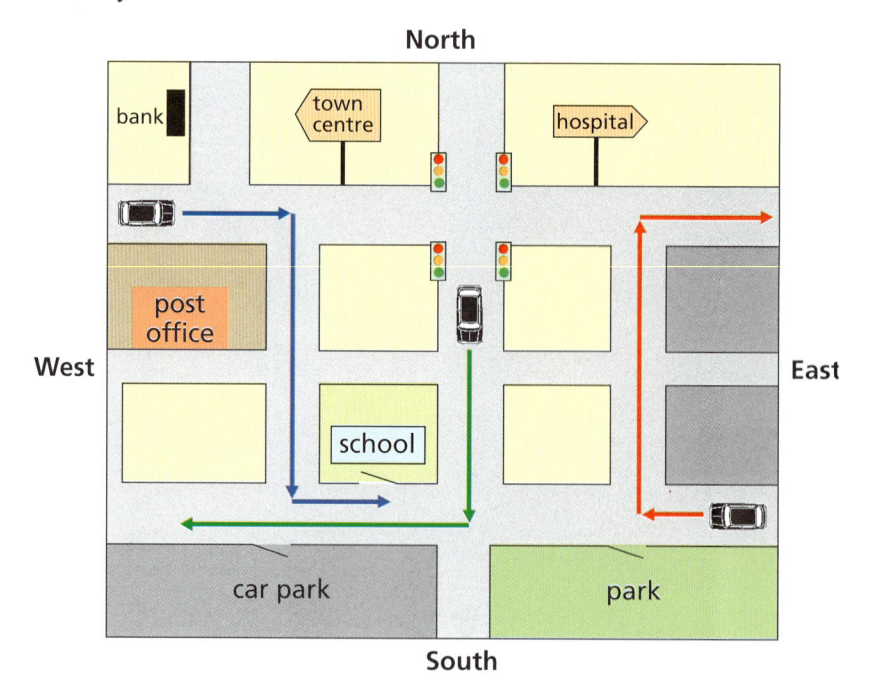

What direction and turns are these cars taking?

Use **N** (North), **S** (South), **E** (East) or **W** (West) to show direction.
Use **RT**$\frac{1}{4}$ (right turn) and **LT**$\frac{1}{4}$ (left turn) to show the turn.

Turns, angles and directions **67**

a) The **green** car is going **S**.
It makes a **RT$\frac{1}{4}$** and goes **W**.

b) The **blue** car is going _____ .
It makes a _____ and goes _____ .
It makes a _____ and goes _____ .

c) The **red** car is going _____ .
It makes a _____ and goes _____ .
It makes a _____ and goes _____ .

12 You may need

- Worksheet 4 *Around town* to help you.

The three cars from **Question 11** go on different journeys around town.
They cannot make a U-turn.
Write the journey each car takes.
Use **N**, **S**, **E**, **W** and **RT$\frac{1}{4}$** or **LT$\frac{1}{4}$**.

a) The **green** car goes to the **post office**.

b) The **red** car goes to the **town centre**.

c) The **blue** car goes to the **park**.

13 Try Worksheet Puzzle *Reach the bank (1), (2)*.

Now try Unit 4 Test.

Review 4

1 a) 6 + 6 = ☐   b) 16 + 6 = ☐

c) 26 + 6 = ☐   d) 36 + 6 = ☐

2

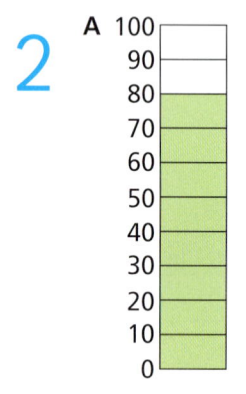

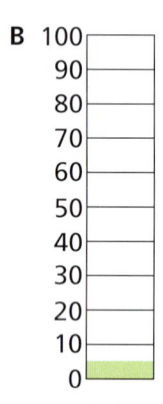

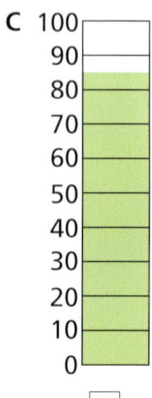

a) **A** = ☐ people   b) **B** = ☐ people   c) **C** = ☐ people

3 a) 10 × 2 = ☐   b) 7 × 10 = ☐

c) 9 × 2 = ☐   d) 5 × 10 = ☐

e) 8 × 2 = ☐   f) 6 × 2 = ☐

g) 10 × 10 = ☐   h) 7 × 2 = ☐

i) 6 × 10 = ☐   j) 1 × 10 = ☐

4 Are these **measures** for **weight** or measures for **liquid** volume?

a) half litre ($\frac{1}{2}$ l) _____

b) gram (g) _____

Review 4 **69**

c) kilogram (kg) _____

d) litre (l) _____

5 Are these **measuring tools** for **weight** or for **liquid** volume?

a) measuring jug _____

b) kitchen scales _____

c) balance scales _____

6 What is the difference in these ages?

a) Twenty years old and five years old?

_____ years

b) Nineteen years old and four years old?

_____ years

c) Twenty years old and six years old?

_____ years

7 Write as decimals:

a) 1 whole and 5 tenths

b) 1 whole and 3 tenths.

5 Number

Multiples of 3, 4 and 5

Unit 5 words

multiply	times	same
group	each	thousand
worth	divide	equal
roughly	left	right

Remember

Examples are shown in red.

 means copy and complete.

You need
- a set of Unit 5 vocabulary Snap cards.

Play a game of Snap to help you learn the words.

Try the **word test** to get some points.

1 a) $2 + 2 + 2 + 2 + 2 = \square$
  5 lots of 2 = $\square$
  $5 \times 2 = \square$

b) $2 + 2 + 2 = \square$
  3 lots of 2 = $\square$
  $3 \times 2 = \square$

Multiples of 3, 4 and 5 • 71

c) $2 + 2 + 2 + 2 + 2 + 2 + 2 = \square$

$7 \times 2 = \square$

d) $10 + 10 + 10 = \square$

$3 \times 10 = \square$

e) $10 + 10 + 10 + 10 + 10 = \square$

$5 \times 10 = \square$

f) $10 + 10 + 10 + 10 + 10 + 10 + 10 + 10 + 10 + 10 = \square$

$10 \times 10 = \square$

2 A B C

a) In group **A** there are $\square$ people; $\square$ eyes $\square$ toes.

b) In group **B** there are $\square$ people; $\square$ eyes $\square$ toes.

c) In group **C** there are $\square$ people; $\square$ eyes $\square$ toes.

3 a) $9 \times 2 = \square$ b) $0 \times 2 = \square$

c) $8 \times 2 = \square$ d) $10 \times 2 = \square$

e) $0 \times 10 = \square$

f) $1 \times 10 = \square$

g) $9 \times 10 = \square$

h) $8 \times 10 = \square$

i) $\square \times 2 = 18$

j) $\square \times 2 = 0$

k) $\square \times 2 = 16$

l) $\square \times 2 = 20$

m) $\square \times 10 = 0$

n) $\square \times 10 = 10$

o) $\square \times 10 = 90$

p) $\square \times 10 = 80$

4 Five friends go out for a meal.

One table seats **5** people.

a) Two tables seat $\square$ people.

b) Three tables seat $\square$ people.

c) Four tables seat $\square$ people.

d) Five tables seat ☐ people.

e) Six tables seat ☐ people.

f) Seven tables seat ☐ people.

g) Eight tables seat ☐ people.

h) Nine tables seat ☐ people.

i) Ten tables seat ☐ people.

5 Try Worksheet 1 *Fives*.

6 How many fingers?

a) 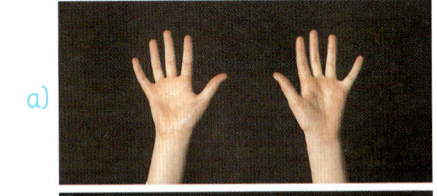 = ☐ fingers

b)  = ☐ fingers

c) 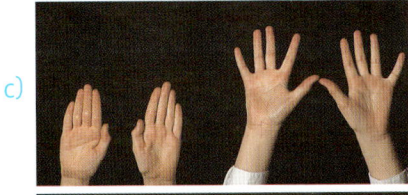 = ☐ fingers

d) 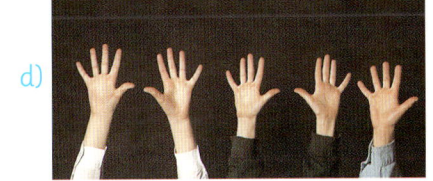 = ☐ fingers

7 Try Worksheet 2 *How many times? (1)*.

Rows of 5

8 You need
- squared paper.

a) $1 \times 5 = \square$ b) $2 \times 5 = \square$ c) $3 \times 5 = \square$

Continue drawing the squares for:

d) $4 \times 5 = \square$ e) $5 \times 5 = \square$ f) $6 \times 5 = \square$

g) $7 \times 5 = \square$ h) $8 \times 5 = \square$ i) $9 \times 5 = \square$

j) $10 \times 5 = \square$

Jumping in 5s

9 1 jump of five, 2 jumps of five

0 1 2 3 4 5 6 7 8 9 10 11 12 13 14 15 16 17 18 19 20

a) 2 jumps of 5 → $2 \times \square$

b) $2 \times 5 = \square$

10 Try Worksheets 3 and 4 *Jumps of five (1), (2)*.

Multiples of 3, 4 and 5   75

11 Here is a ×5 number machine.
When you put a number in, it multiplies it by 5.

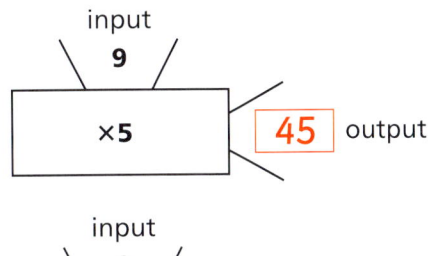

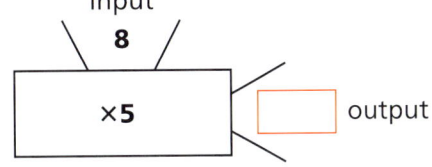

input **9** → ×5 → **45** output

input **8** → ×5 → ☐ output

a) The **output** number is ☐.

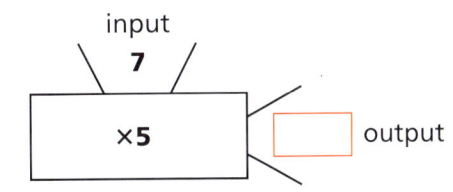

input **7** → ×5 → ☐ output

b) The **output** number is ☐.

c) Draw a machine for input **2** and a machine for input **3**.

12 Try Worksheet 5 *Number machines*.

13
a) 6 × 5 = ☐   b) 0 × 5 = ☐   c) 5 × 5 = ☐

d) 4 × 5 = ☐   e) 9 × 5 = ☐   f) 7 × 5 = ☐

g) ☐ × 5 = 30   h) ☐ × 5 = 0   i) ☐ × 5 = 25

j) ☐ × 5 = 20   k) ☐ × 5 = 45   l) ☐ × 5 = 35

UNIT 5 NUMBER

14 Look at the pair of dot patterns below.

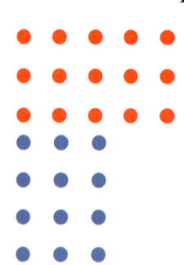

Three rows of five make fifteen.

Five rows of three make fifteen.

Three rows of **five** and **five** rows of **three** give the same answer.

a) $3 \times 5 = \square$

b) $5 \times 3 = \square$

c) Draw the dots to make your own **pattern pairs** for 2×5, 4×5 and 6×5.

15 Five friends go camping.

If they **each** need:

a) They will have to take $\square$ tins of beans altogether.

Multiples of 3, 4 and 5 • 77

b) They will have to take ☐ bags altogether.

c) They will have to take ☐ rolls altogether.

d) They will have to take ☐ apples altogether.

e) They will have to take ☐ cans altogether.

f) They will have to take ☐ packets of crisps altogether.

UNIT 5 NUMBER

16 🍀 **One** four-leaf clover = **4** leaves.

a) 🍀🍀 **Two** four-leaf clovers = ☐ leaves.

b) 🍀🍀🍀 **Three** four-leaf clovers = ☐ leaves.

c) 🍀🍀🍀🍀 **Four** four-leaf clovers = ☐ leaves.

d) 🍀🍀🍀🍀🍀 **Five** four-leaf clovers = ☐ leaves.

17 △ **One** triangle = **3** sides.

a) △△ **Two** triangles = ☐ sides.

b) △△△ **Three** triangles = ☐ sides.

c) △△△△ **Four** triangles = ☐ sides.

d) △△△△△ **Five** triangles = ☐ sides.

18 Try Worksheet 6 *How many times? (2)*.

Multiples of 3, 4 and 5 · 79

Rows of 4

19 You need
- squared paper.

a) $1 \times 4 = \square$ b) $2 \times 4 = \square$  c) $3 \times 4 = \square$

Continue drawing the squares for:

d) $4 \times 4 = \square$ e) $5 \times 4 = \square$

Rows of 3

20 You need
- squared paper.

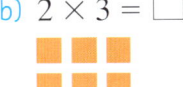

a) $1 \times 3 = \square$ b) $2 \times 3 = \square$ c) $3 \times 3 = \square$

Continue drawing the squares for:

d) $4 \times 3 = \square$ e) $5 \times 3 = \square$

21 Try Worksheet 7 *Jumps of three and four*.

22 Here is a ×4 number machine.
When you put a number in, it multiplies it by 4.

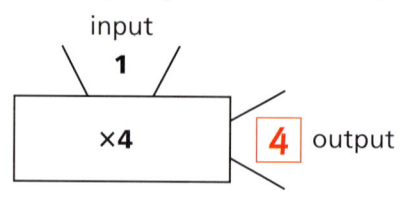

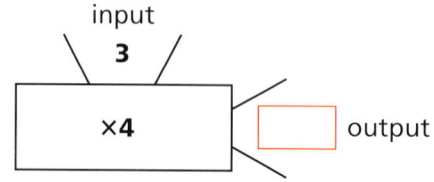

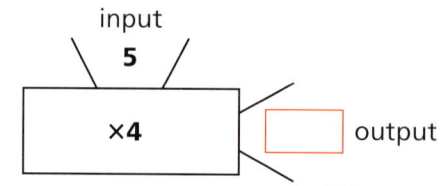

input: 1 → ×4 → output: 4

input: 3 → ×4 → output: ☐

a) The **output** number is ☐.

input: 5 → ×4 → output: ☐

b) The **output** number is ☐.

c) Make up some ×3 number machines.

23 a) $\boxed{3} \times 4 = 12$

b) ☐ × 4 = 4   c) ☐ × 4 = 8

d) ☐ × 4 = 20   e) ☐ × 4 = 16

f) ☐ × 3 = 6   g) ☐ × 3 = 12

h) ☐ × 3 = 3   i) ☐ × 3 = 9

Multiples of 3, 4 and 5 • 81

24 Look at the pair of dot patterns below.

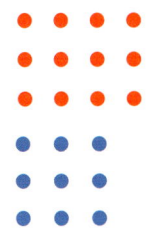

Three rows of **four** make **twelve**.

Four rows of **three** make **twelve**.

Three rows of **four** and **four** rows of **three** give the same answer.

a) 3 × 4 = ☐   b) 4 × 3 = ☐

c) Draw the dots to make your own **pattern pairs** for 2 × 4 and 5 × 4.

25 Look at the pair of dot patterns below.

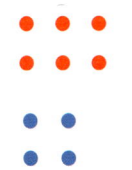

Two rows of **three** make **six**.

Three rows of **two** make **six**.

Three rows of **two** and **two** rows of **three** give the same answer.

a) 2 × 3 = ☐   b) 3 × 2 = ☐

c) Draw the dots to make your own **pattern pairs** for 4 × 3 and 5 × 3.

82 UNIT 5 NUMBER

26
a) Five cars = _____ wheels.

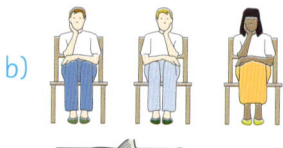

b) Four rows = _____ people.

c) Seven fish = _____ kg.

d) Nine rows = _____ lettuces.

e) Eight stamps = _____ pence.

f) Four stamps = _____ pence.

g) Five stamps = _____ pence.

h) Ten stamps = _____ pence

or _____ pound.

27 Make up your own problems for:

5 × 5   3 × 4   2 × 3

Make a display.

28 You need
- Unit 5 Race against time cards
- your 'My maths record' sheet.

Multiples of 3, 4 and 5

Race against time

1 Sort the race cards – this side up.

2×5

2 Take the cards one at a time.

3 Answer as quickly as you can.

4 Did you get it right?
Look at the other side of the card.

10

5 When you get all the answers correct, ask a friend to test you.

6 Now **Race against time**.

Go for points!

Ask your teacher to test and time you.

Remember

3 errors – 1 point

2 errors – 2 points

1 error – 3 points

0 errors – 5 points

Answer in 1 minute with 0 errors – 7 points

Now try Unit 5 Test.

Review 5

1 Sam is 17 years old. His brother Tom is 8 years **older**.
Tom is ☐ years old.

2 Write the **value** of the 2 – **thousands**, **hundreds**, **tens** or **units**.

a) 1 ② 9

_____

b) 9 ②

_____

c) 1 ② 1 9

_____

d) ② 1 9 1

_____

3 a) Do you use a **metre**, a **kilogram** or a **litre** measure to find out how much milk to use in cooking?

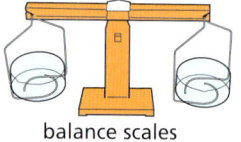

I use a _____ .

b) Do you use [balance scales] [measuring jug] [measuring tape] to find out how much milk to use in cooking?

I use a _____ .

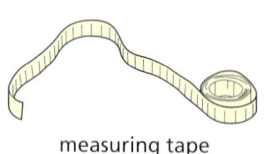

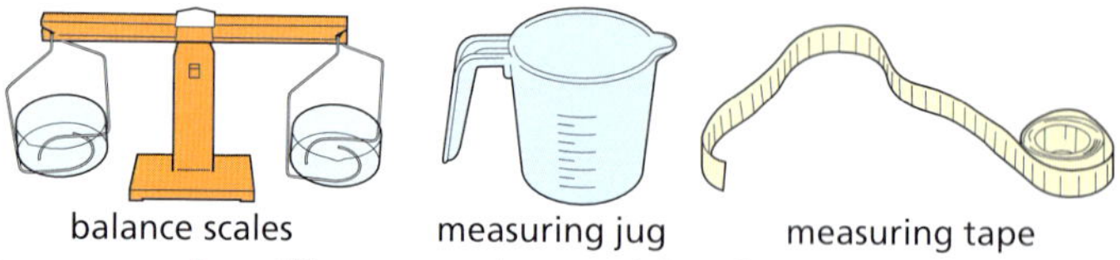

4 Write down the missing numbers.

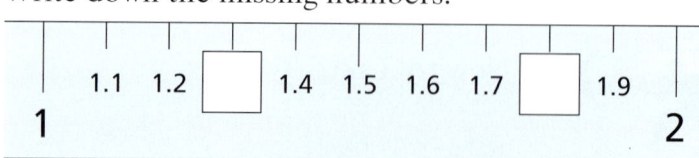

1 | 1.1 | 1.2 | ☐ | 1.4 | 1.5 | 1.6 | 1.7 | ☐ | 1.9 | 2

Review 5 • 85

5 Draw the boxes and colour in to show the **decimal numbers**.

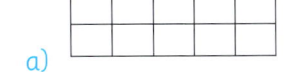

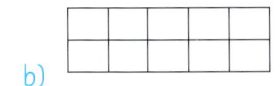

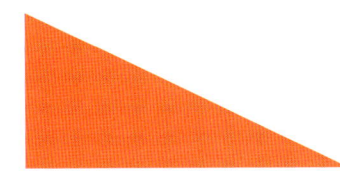

a) 0.4

b) 0.6

6 How are these two shapes alike?

7 To help me remember, my:

a) 30 cm reminder is _____ .

b) 1 m reminder is _____ .

c) 1 kg reminder is _____ .

d) ½ l reminder is _____ .

8 a) 20 − 8 = ☐   b) 20 − ☐ = 8

c) 20 − ☐ = 12

6 Shape and space

2D and 3D shapes

Unit 6 words

line	pentagon	shape
symmetry	square	rectangle
triangle	circle	cube
cuboid	sphere	cylinder

Remember

Examples are shown in red

means copy and complete.

You need
- a set of Unit 6 vocabulary Snap cards.

Play a game of Snap to help you learn the words.

Try the **word test** to get some points.

Symmetry

This scene has a mirror line.

It has a **line of symmetry**.

This house has a mirror line.

Some letters have a **line of symmetry**.

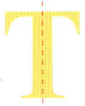

T B

1 Write out the capital letters of the alphabet.

A B C D E F G H I J K L M
N O P Q R S T U V W X Y Z

a) Draw a **line of symmetry** on the **symmetrical** letters.

b) Can you put **two** lines of symmetry on any letters?

UNIT 6 SHAPE AND SPACE

2 Try Worksheet 1 *Letter lines*.

3 This apple is symmetrical.

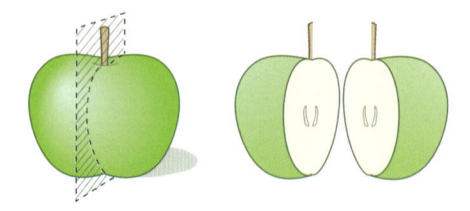

> **Remember**
>
> If something can be cut into two **equal** parts which **mirror** each other we say it is **symmetrical**.

A line is drawn where these objects will be cut.
Do the cuts show that the objects are **symmetrical**?

Answer **Yes** or **No**.

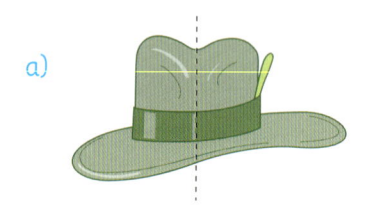

a) b)

4 Try Worksheet 2 *2D and 3D symmetry*.

5 You need
- a cube.

In maths we show hidden **faces** on a 3D shape with broken lines − − − − − − .

2D and 3D shapes 89

see-through cube

faces we can **really** see

a) We **can** see ☐ square faces.

b) We can **not** see ☐ other square faces.

see-through cuboid

faces we can **really** see

c) We **can** see ☐ rectangular faces.

d) We can **not** see ☐ rectangular faces.

6 Try Worksheet 3 *Draw the hidden faces.*

7 a) A cube has ☐ square faces.

b) A cuboid has ☐ rectangular faces.

8 You need
- a set of 2D and 3D shapes.

Play a game of 'Guess the shape'.

Rules for 'Guess the shape'

1 Player A thinks of one of the shapes but does not say which one.

2 Player B asks questions to guess the shape. But the questions can only be answered 'Yes' or 'No'.

3 Player A answers Yes or No and records the number of questions player B uses to guess the shape correctly.

4 Players change over.

5 Player B thinks of a shape.

6 Player A asks questions to guess the shape.

7 The winner is the player who needed fewer questions to guess the shape.

....

Questions you might ask to guess the shape

Is it 3D? Is it symmetrical? Does it have 4 sides? Is it a square?

9 How many **triangles** are there in the shape below?

There are ☐ triangles.

2D and 3D shapes 91

10 Try Worksheet 4 *Find the shapes*.

11 a) Find out how many smaller triangles there are in this large triangle. You can use Worksheet 5 to help you.

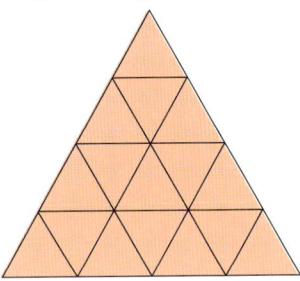

b) Find out how many smaller squares there are in this large square.

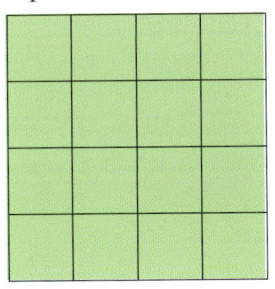

12 a) How many pentagons?

5 groups of ☐ pentagons = ☐ pentagons.
3 groups of ☐ pentagons = ☐ pentagons.

b) How many squares?

5 groups of ☐ squares = ☐ squares.
8 groups of ☐ squares = ☐ squares.

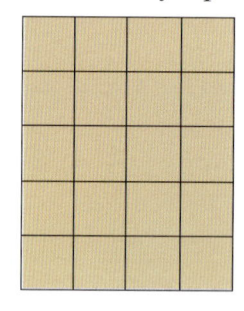

c) How many squares?

5 groups of ☐ squares = ☐ squares.
4 groups of ☐ squares = ☐ squares.

Draw these groups of shapes and try to fit them together like **Question 12c**.

d) squares for 10 × 2

e) rectangles for 5 × 7

f) circles for 3 × 4

g) Which shape did you find hardest to fit together?

2D and 3D shapes

13 You need
- a box of 2D shapes.

Some shapes fit together with no gaps.

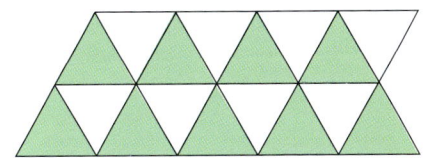

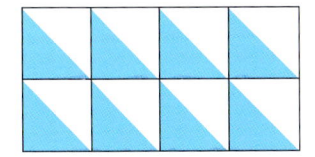

or

Find other shapes which fit together with no gaps.
Make patterns by drawing round them.

14 Look at this football.

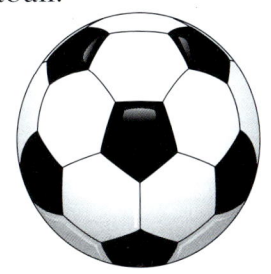

You can see _____ and _____ shapes.

15 How many more **square** and **triangle** tiles would be needed to fill this tiled wall?

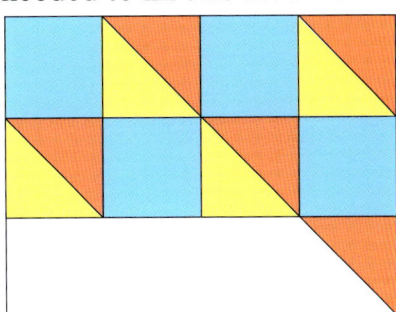

☐ more square tiles and ☐ more triangle tiles are needed.

94 UNIT 6 SHAPE AND SPACE

16 Bathrooms are tiled so that water cannot get between the tiles.

Can you use other shapes to design a more interesting pattern for a bathroom wall?

You can use Worksheet Puzzle *Tile a bathroom (1)*, *(2)* to help you.

Now try Unit 6 Test.

Review 6

1 a) 46 people on the bus. 16 more get on. How many now?

b) 46 people on the bus. 8 get off. How many left?

2 1 block stands for 10 people.
Draw and **colour** the **columns** so that:

a) **A** shows 40

b) **B** shows 45

c) **C** shows 90

d) **D** shows 95

3 🧍 = 10 people

a) 🧍 = ☐ people

b) 🧍🧍 = ☐ people

UNIT 6 SHAPE AND SPACE

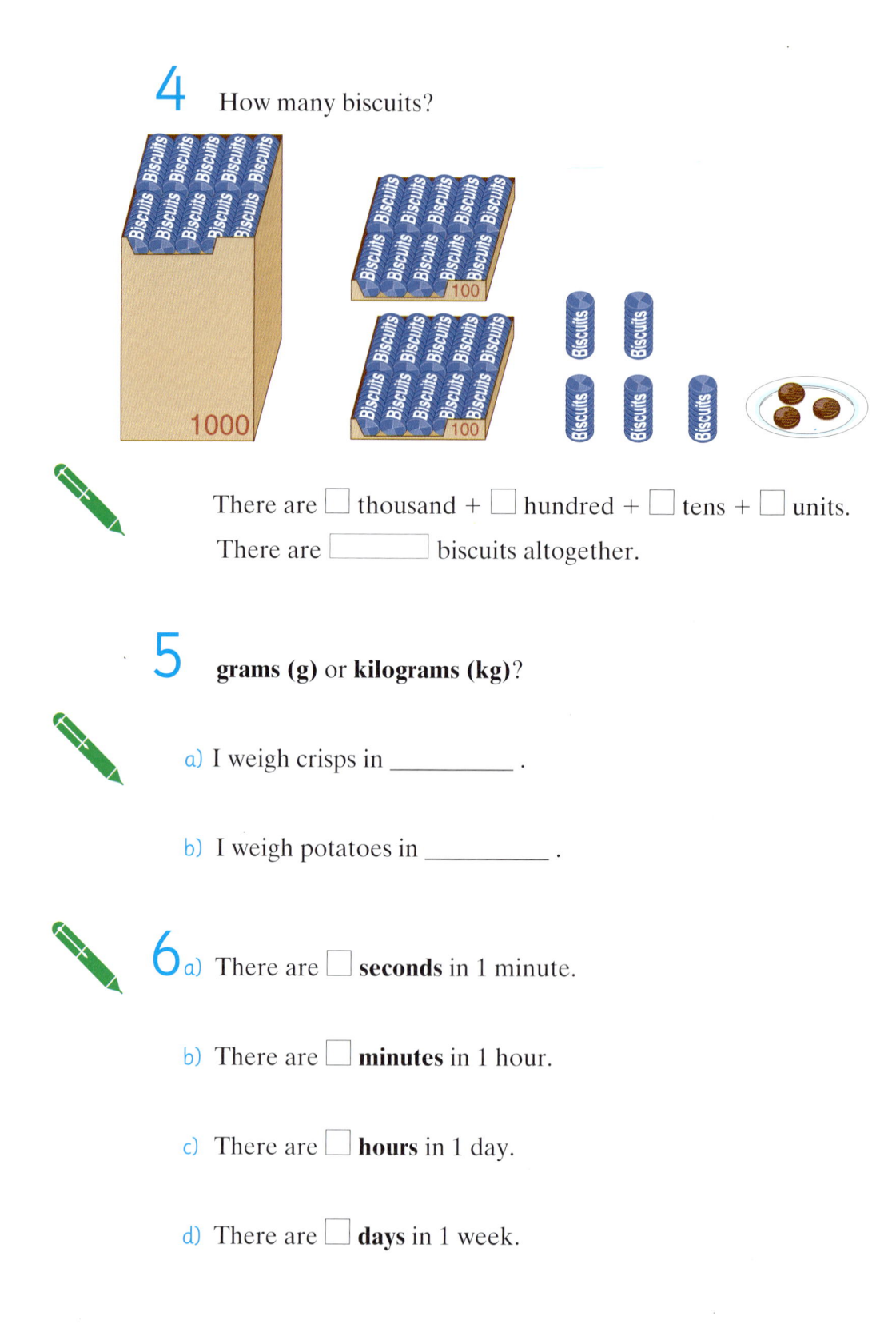

4 How many biscuits?

There are ☐ thousand + ☐ hundred + ☐ tens + ☐ units.

There are ☐ biscuits altogether.

5 **grams (g)** or **kilograms (kg)**?

a) I weigh crisps in _____ .

b) I weigh potatoes in _____ .

6 a) There are ☐ **seconds** in 1 minute.

b) There are ☐ **minutes** in 1 hour.

c) There are ☐ **hours** in 1 day.

d) There are ☐ **days** in 1 week.

7 a) 6 ÷ 2   b) 7 ÷ 2   c) 14 ÷ 2

   d) 15 ÷ 2   e) 50 ÷ 10   f) 56 ÷ 10

8 Put in order – **smallest** decimal first.
   0.5   0.1   0.9   0.7   1.0

7 Number

Decimal fractions

Unit 7 words

fraction	nought	scale
pounds	pence	amount
whole	tenth	decimal
quarter	half	value

> **Remember**
> Examples are shown in red.
>
> ✎ means copy and complete.

You need
- a set of Unit 7 vocabulary Snap cards.

Play a game of Snap to help you learn the words.

Try the **word test** to get some points.

1 How much rock is in each picture?
Write as a **fraction** and as a **decimal**.

> **Remember**
> A **decimal point** separates the
> **whole numbers** from the **fractions**.

Decimal fractions • 99

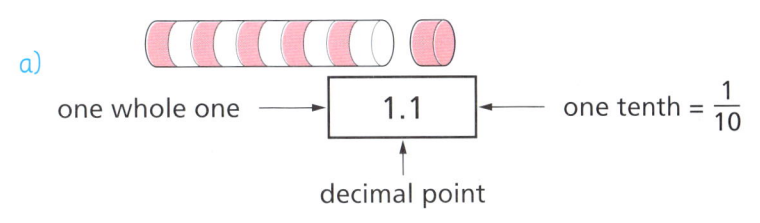

a)
one whole one → 1.1 ← one tenth = $\frac{1}{10}$
decimal point

a) $1\frac{1}{10} = 1.1$

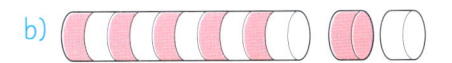

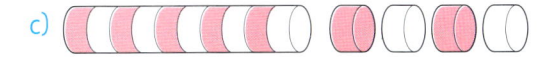

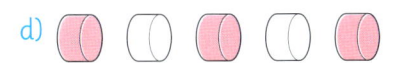

b)

c)

d)

e)

f) How many more ways can you write **one**?

one or **1** or **1 whole** or **1 unit**

2
What fraction of these towels is coloured **red**?
What fraction is coloured **green**?
Write each as a **fraction** and as a **decimal**.

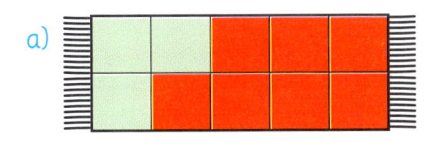

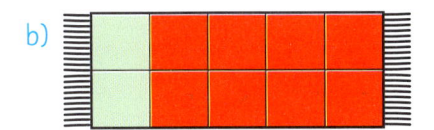

a)

b)

a) **red** $\frac{7}{10} = 0.7$
   green $\frac{3}{10} = 0.3$

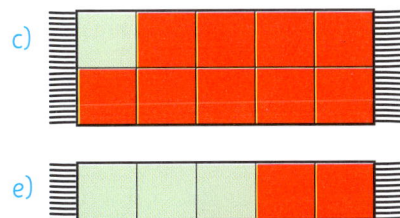

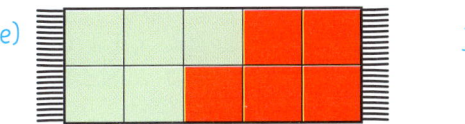

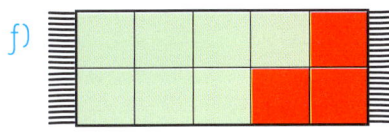

c)

d)

e)

f)

UNIT 7 NUMBER

3 Try Worksheet 1 *Links*.

4 You need
- a calculator.

Enter `0.1` into your calculator to start **each** line of numbers.

> **Remember**
>
> Press A/C to cancel after each line.

Your partner guesses what the **first** answer in line a) will be.
You press = to see if your partner is right.
Then add on each of the next numbers, in turn.
Ask your partner to guess each answer.

Take turns to do lines b), c) and d).

a) + 1 = ☐ + 1 = ☐ + 1 = ☐ + 1 = ☐ + 1 = ☐

b) + 0.1 = ☐ + 0.1 = ☐ + 0.1 = ☐ + 0.1 = ☐ + 0.1 = ☐

c) + 0.1 = ☐ + 1 = ☐ + 0.1 = ☐ + 1 = ☐ + 0.1 = ☐

d) + 0.5 = ☐ + 0.1 = ☐ + 0.1 = ☐ + 0.1 = ☐ + 0.1 = ☐

e) Enter `0.9` in your calculator.
What do you think it will show if you add `0.1` ?
Check it out.
Now try:

f) 1.9 + 0.1   g) 3.9 + 0.1   h) 9.9 + 0.1

Decimal fractions 101

5 Draw the speech bubbles.
Fill in the **missing words** in the **empty bubbles**.

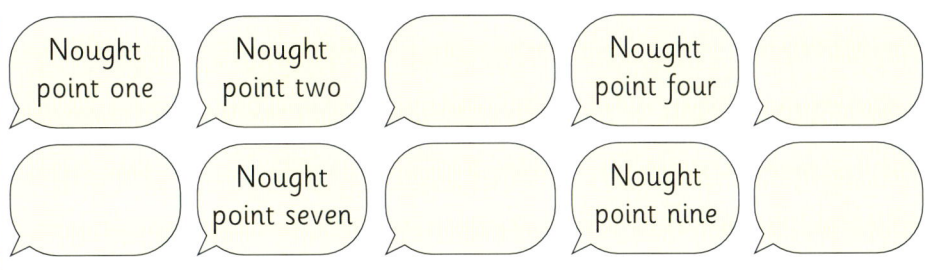

- Nought point one
- Nought point two
-
- Nought point four
-
-
- Nought point seven
-
- Nought point nine
-

6 Look at the ruler.
If we look through a magnifying glass at 1 cm–2 cm

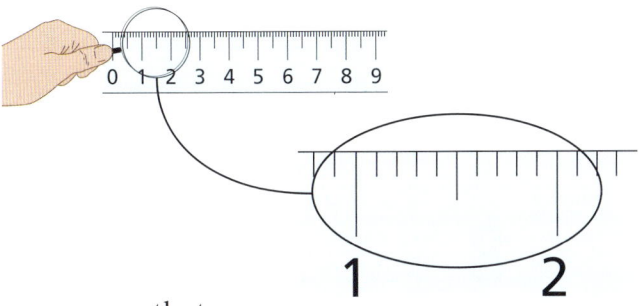

we can see that:
each centimetre is divided into **10** equal parts
each part is **one tenth** of a centimetre $\frac{1}{10}$.

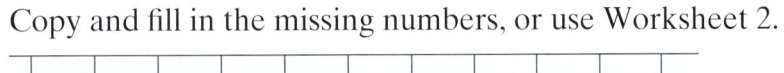

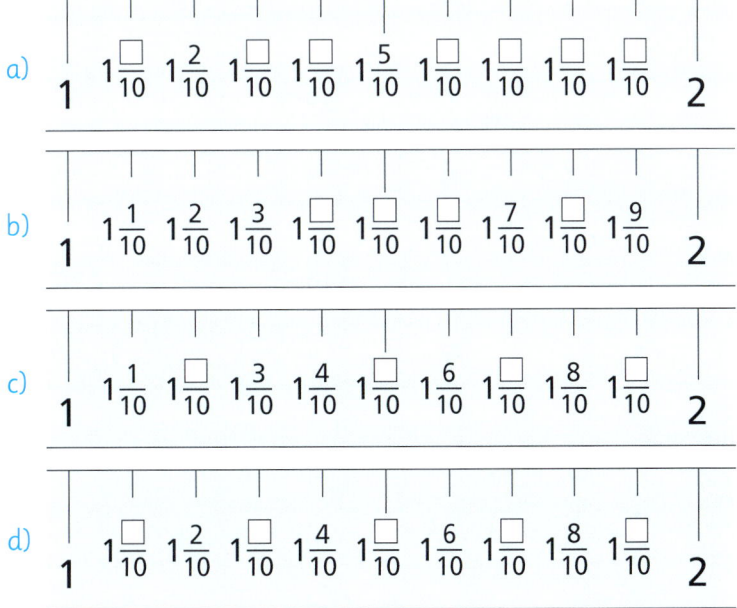

Copy and fill in the missing numbers, or use Worksheet 2.

a) 1, $1\frac{\square}{10}$, $1\frac{2}{10}$, $1\frac{\square}{10}$, $1\frac{\square}{10}$, $1\frac{5}{10}$, $1\frac{\square}{10}$, $1\frac{\square}{10}$, $1\frac{\square}{10}$, $1\frac{\square}{10}$, 2

b) 1, $1\frac{1}{10}$, $1\frac{2}{10}$, $1\frac{3}{10}$, $1\frac{\square}{10}$, $1\frac{\square}{10}$, $1\frac{\square}{10}$, $1\frac{7}{10}$, $1\frac{\square}{10}$, $1\frac{9}{10}$, 2

c) 1, $1\frac{1}{10}$, $1\frac{\square}{10}$, $1\frac{3}{10}$, $1\frac{4}{10}$, $1\frac{\square}{10}$, $1\frac{6}{10}$, $1\frac{\square}{10}$, $1\frac{8}{10}$, $1\frac{\square}{10}$, 2

d) 1, $1\frac{\square}{10}$, $1\frac{2}{10}$, $1\frac{\square}{10}$, $1\frac{4}{10}$, $1\frac{\square}{10}$, $1\frac{6}{10}$, $1\frac{\square}{10}$, $1\frac{8}{10}$, $1\frac{\square}{10}$, 2

UNIT 7 NUMBER

7 Fill in the missing decimals, or use Worksheet 2.

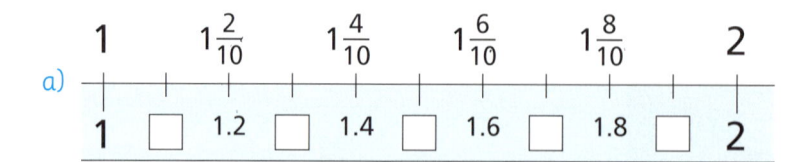

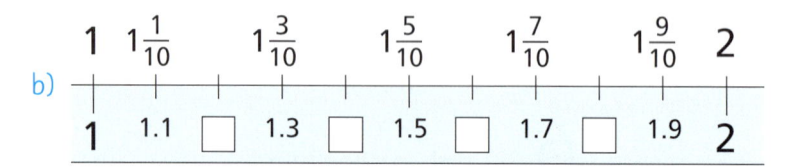

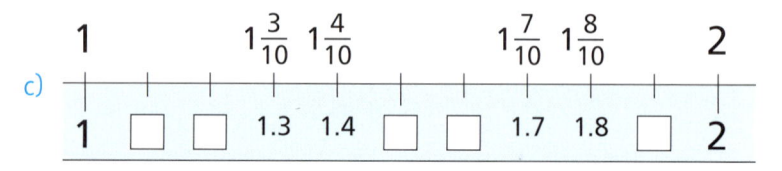

a)
Top: 1, $1\frac{2}{10}$, $1\frac{4}{10}$, $1\frac{6}{10}$, $1\frac{8}{10}$, 2
Bottom: 1, ☐, 1.2, ☐, 1.4, ☐, 1.6, ☐, 1.8, ☐, 2

b)
Top: 1, $1\frac{1}{10}$, $1\frac{3}{10}$, $1\frac{5}{10}$, $1\frac{7}{10}$, $1\frac{9}{10}$, 2
Bottom: 1, 1.1, ☐, 1.3, ☐, 1.5, ☐, 1.7, ☐, 1.9, 2

c)
Top: 1, $1\frac{3}{10}$, $1\frac{4}{10}$, $1\frac{7}{10}$, $1\frac{8}{10}$, 2
Bottom: 1, ☐, ☐, 1.3, 1.4, ☐, ☐, 1.7, 1.8, ☐, 2

8 Now try these.

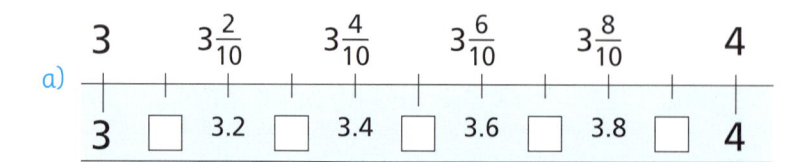

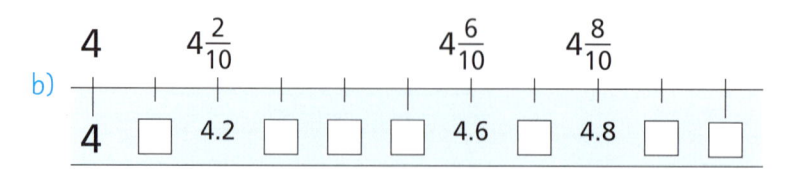

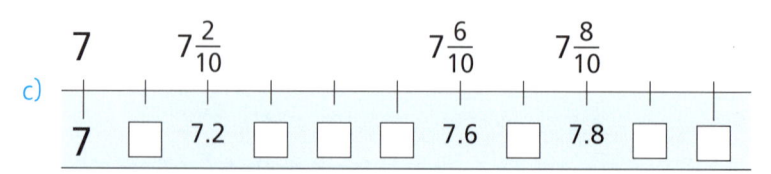

a)
Top: 3, $3\frac{2}{10}$, $3\frac{4}{10}$, $3\frac{6}{10}$, $3\frac{8}{10}$, 4
Bottom: 3, ☐, 3.2, ☐, 3.4, ☐, 3.6, ☐, 3.8, ☐, 4

b)
Top: 4, $4\frac{2}{10}$, $4\frac{6}{10}$, $4\frac{8}{10}$
Bottom: 4, ☐, 4.2, ☐, ☐, ☐, 4.6, ☐, 4.8, ☐, ☐

c)
Top: 7, $7\frac{2}{10}$, $7\frac{6}{10}$, $7\frac{8}{10}$
Bottom: 7, ☐, 7.2, ☐, ☐, ☐, 7.6, ☐, 7.8, ☐, ☐

Decimal fractions 103

9 Write the next decimal number going **up** the scale.

a) 0.5 → ☐.☐ b) 0.8 → ☐.☐ c) 0.9 → ☐.☐ d) 1.0 → ☐.☐ e) 1.8 → ☐.☐

f) 1.9 → ☐.☐ g) 2.0 → ☐.☐ h) 3.0 → ☐.☐ i) 4.0 → ☐.☐

10 Write the next decimal number going **down** the scale.

a) 0.6 → ☐.☐ b) 0.9 → ☐.☐ c) 1.0 → ☐.☐ d) 1.1 → ☐.☐ e) 1.9 → ☐.☐

f) 2.0 → ☐.☐ g) 2.1 → ☐.☐ h) 3.1 → ☐.☐ i) 4.1 → ☐.☐

11 Try Worksheet 3 *Line up*.

12 Look at these parts of a ruler.
Which number does the arrow point to each time?

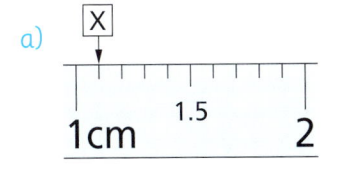

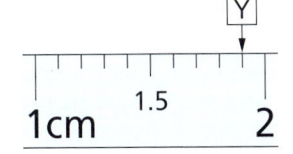

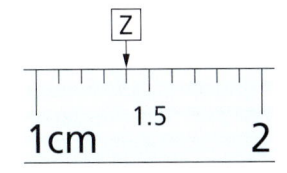

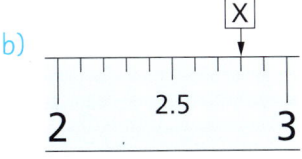

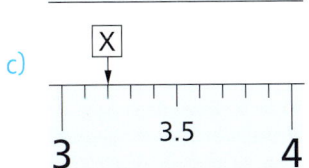

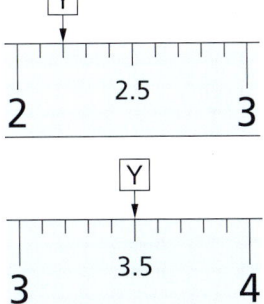

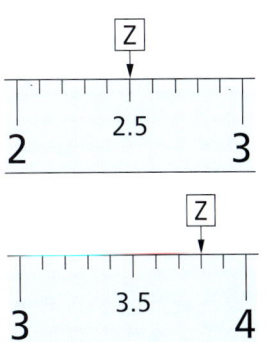

a) X = 1.1 cm   Y = 1.9 cm   Z = 1.4 cm

b)

c)

13 How long are these pencils?

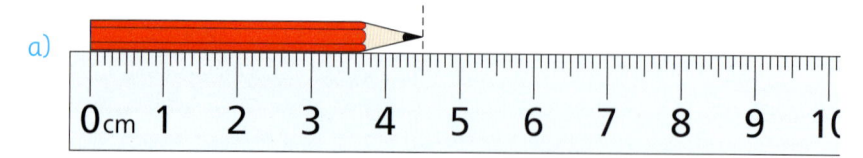

a) **4.5 cm**

b)

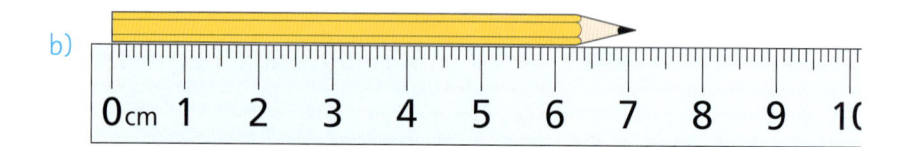

c)

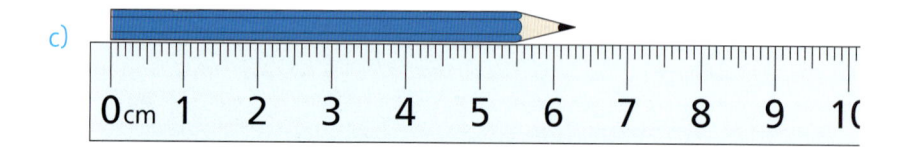

d)

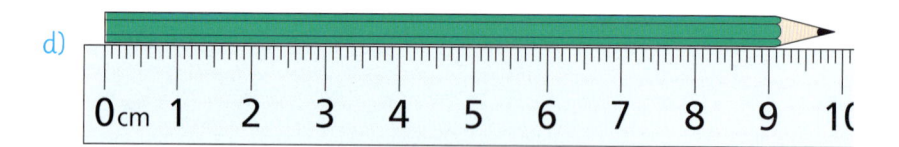

14 You need
- a calculator.

Put these **decimal numbers** into the calculator. Write down the answers.

a) 4.1 + 0.9 b) 2.2 + 0.8 c) 9.3 + 0.7

d) 9.4 + 0.6 e) 5.5 + 0.5 f) 9.6 + 0.4

g) 3.7 + 0.3 h) 8.8 + 0.2 i) 9.9 + 0.1

j) What do you notice about all the answers?

Decimal fractions 105

15 Try Worksheet 4 *Different decimals*.

16 You need
- one set of 'Speed sort' cards each. (Do not mix the sets up.)
- a stop-watch.

Play a game of 'Speed sort'.

> **Rules for 'Speed sort'**
> 1 Both shuffle your set of cards.
> 2 Look at line **A** below.
> 3 See how quickly you and your partner can:
>   a) find the cards
>   b) put them in order, **smallest** number first.
> 4 The first player with a set of cards in order is the winner.
> 5 Then try line **B**, then line **C**, then line **D**.

A | 0.8 | 0.2 | 0.6 | 0.3 | 0.7 |

B | 1.8 | 1.3 | 1.7 | 1.0 | 1.9 |

C | 0.1 | 1.4 | 1.1 | 0.5 | 1.6 |

D | 3.5 | 1.5 | 2.5 | 0.4 | 2.0 |

17

You need
- base 10 blocks.

Sue works in a shop at weekends.

She keeps some single biscuits on a plate for people to taste.

There are ten single biscuits in one packet.

There are ten packets in boxes marked 100.

Sue divides **one** biscuit into **ten equal parts**.

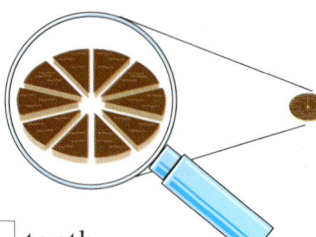

a) Each small part of the biscuit is ☐ tenth.

b) ☐ small parts make **1** whole biscuit.

Decimal fractions • 107

c) ☐ **tenths** make **1 unit**.

d) ☐ **single biscuits** make **1 packet of ten**.

e) ☐ **units** make **1 ten**.

f) ☐ **packets of ten** make **1 box of a hundred**.

g) ☐ **tens** make **1 hundred**.

18 Try Worksheet 5 *Ten of these make?*

19 What is the value of the circled digit – **tens**, **units** or **tenths**?

(4) 0   **tens**   (4) . 0   **units**   0 . (4)   **tenths**

a) (2) 0 . 0   b) (2) 0   c) 0 . (2)

d) 4 3 . (2)   e) (2) 4 . 3   f) 4 (2) . 3

g) (3) 2 . 4   h) 4 (3) . 2

i) 2 4 . (3)   j) 0 . (3)

k) 12.3 = ☐ ten ☐ units ☐ tenths.

l) 32.1 = ☐ tens ☐ units ☐ tenths.

m) 20.1 = ☐ tens ☐ units ☐ tenths.

UNIT 7 NUMBER

20 Fill in the missing words – **tens**, **units** or **tenths**.

a) 3 = three _____

b) 4.3 = four _____ three _____ .

c) 40 = four _____ no _____ .

d) 3.4 = three _____ four _____ .

e) 34.2 = three _____ four _____ two _____ .

f) 50.4 = five _____ no _____ four _____ .

21 We also use the **decimal point** to separate **pounds** from **pence**.
We write:

100p as **£1.00**

120p as **£1.20**

125p as one whole **pound** → **£1 . 25** ← twenty-five **pence**.
                                        ↑
                                  decimal point

How much money in each picture?
Use the **£** sign and the **decimal point**.

a) ↑   ↑

a)   £1 . 20

Decimal fractions 109

b) _____

c) _____

d) _____

e) _____

f) _____

g) _____

22 Write down **only** the amounts below which are written **correctly**.

> **Remember**
> Never use the £ and the p signs at the same time.

a) £124p b) 123p c) £2.16 d) £3.43p

e) £5.48p f) £2.50 g) £328p h) £8.12

UNIT 7 NUMBER

23
Write these amounts in pounds.
Use the £ sign.

> **Remember**
> Don't use £ and p at the same time.

a) 145p   b) 235p

a) £1.45   b) £2.35

c) 360p   d) 421p

e) 524p   f) 980p

g) 321p   h) 382p

i) 351p   j) 920p

24
You need
- a calculator.

Carol and Bob go on holiday.
They buy some things from the Beach Shop.

Map	35p
Rock	68p
Stamps	27p
Postcards	25p
Ice-cream	75p
Lolly	24p
Crisps	26p

Sandals	£1.45
Bucket	73p
Spade	49p
Hat	£1.80
Glasses	£5.45
Sun-cream	£2.28
T-shirt	£2.20
Shorts	£3.50

Decimal fractions 111

What would Carol pay if she buys:

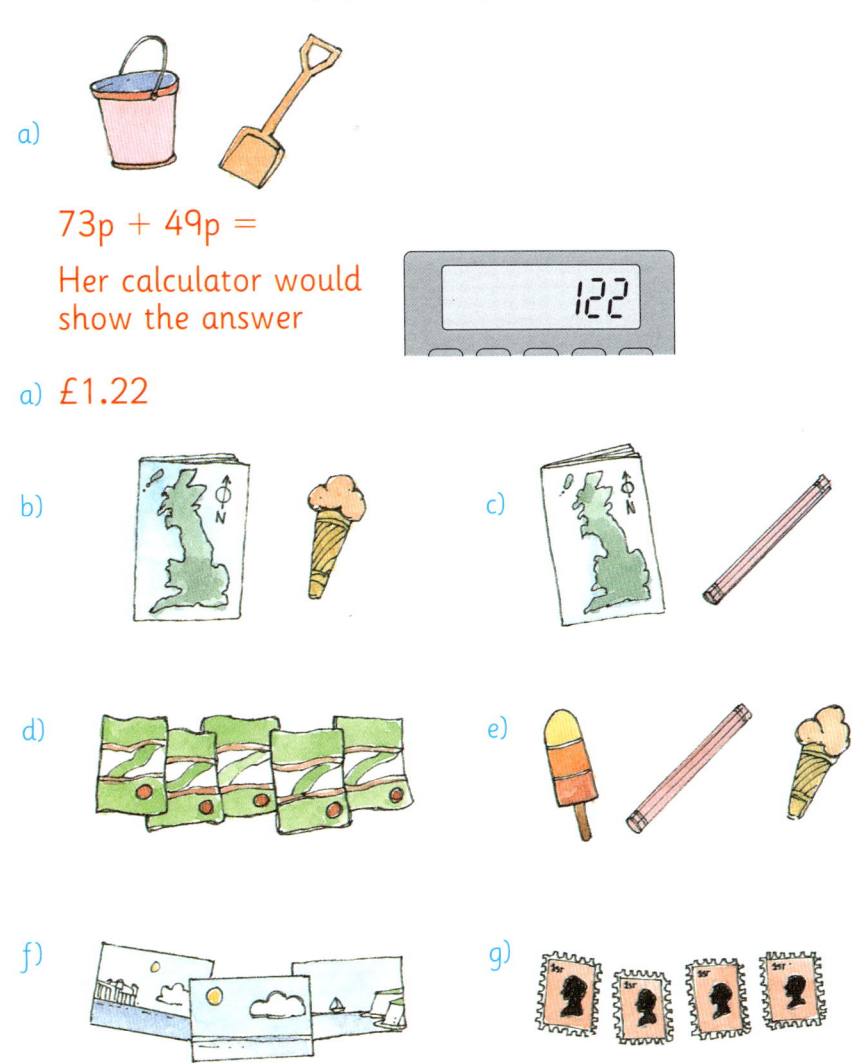

a)

73p + 49p =

Her calculator would show the answer | 1.22 |

a) £1.22

b)

c)

d)

e)

f)

g)

h) Which is the **cheapest** bill Carol would have to pay?

i) Which is the **dearest** bill Carol would have to pay?

UNIT 7 NUMBER

25 What would Bob pay if he buys these from the Beach Shop?

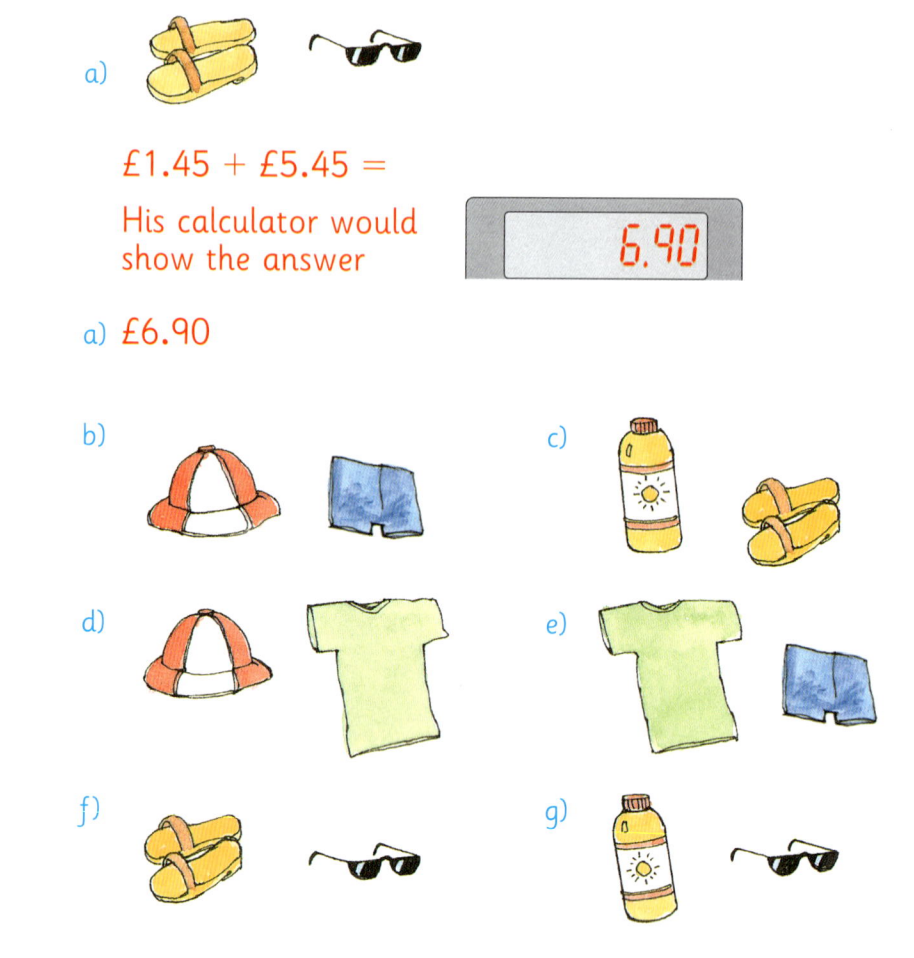

a)

£1.45 + £5.45 =

His calculator would show the answer **6.90**

a) £6.90

b)

c)

d)

e)

f)

g)

h) Which is the **cheapest** bill Bob would have to pay?

i) Which is the **dearest** bill Bob would have to pay?

j) Find the largest number of **different** things they could buy if they had:

　i) £5.00　　ii) £10.00

26 You need

- Unit 7 Race against time cards
- your 'My maths record' sheet.

Race against time

1 Sort the race cards (Set 1) – this side up.

[card: 9.1]

2 Take the cards **one** at a time.

3 Answer as quickly as you can: 'One tenth'.

4 Did you get it right? Look at the other side of the card.

[card: 1 tenth]

5 When you get all the answers correct, ask a friend to test you.

6 Now **Race against time**.

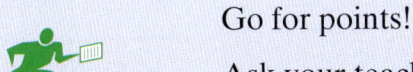

Go for points!

Ask your teacher to test and time you.

7 Now try again with Set 2 – this side up.

[card: 4.5]

8 Race against time and go for more points.

Remember

3 errors – 1 point

2 errors – 2 points

1 error – 3 points

0 errors – 5 points

Answer in 1 minute with 0 errors – 7 points

Now try Unit 7 Test.

Review 7

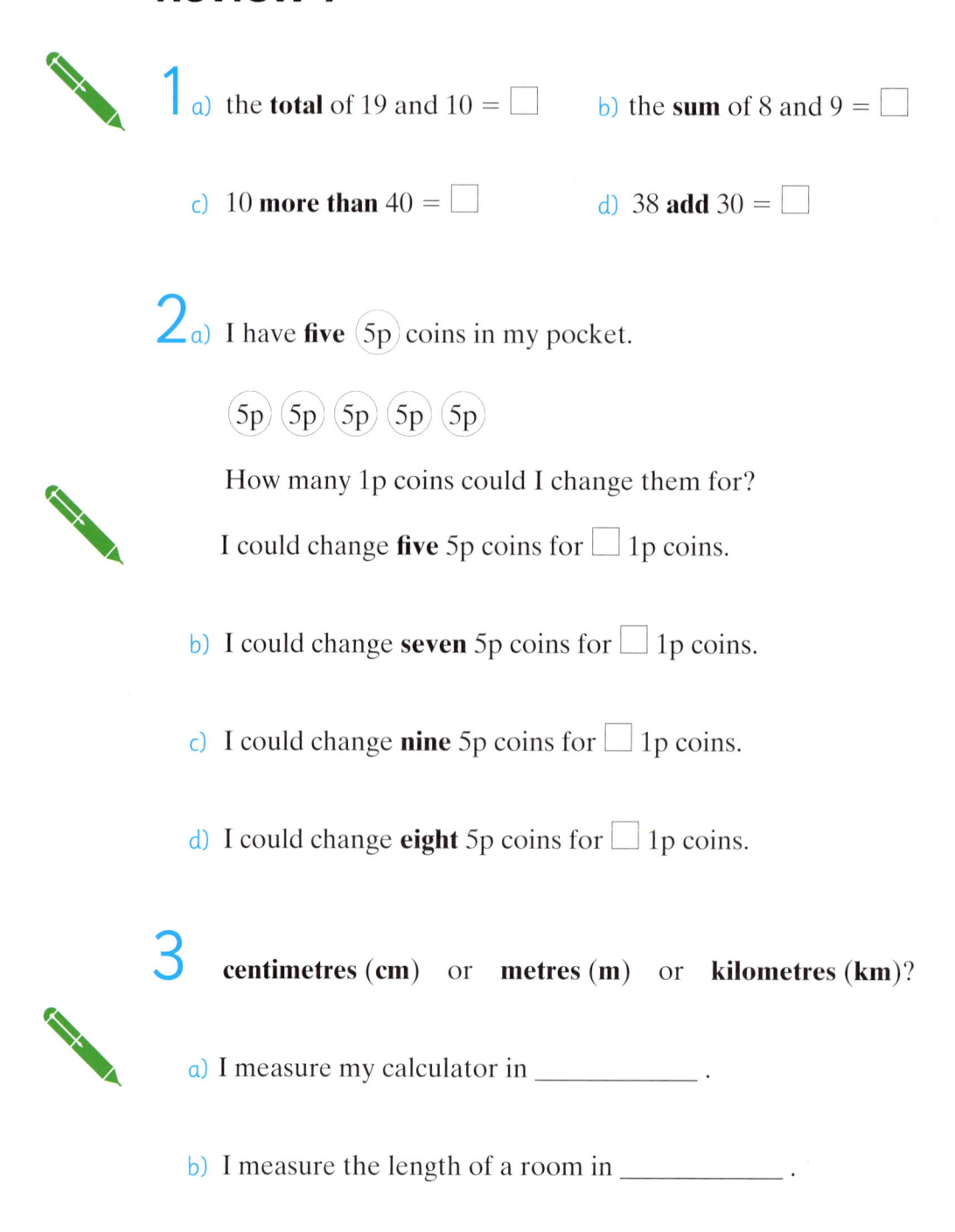

1
a) the **total** of 19 and 10 = ☐
b) the **sum** of 8 and 9 = ☐

c) 10 **more than** 40 = ☐
d) 38 **add** 30 = ☐

2
a) I have **five** 5p coins in my pocket.

5p 5p 5p 5p 5p

How many 1p coins could I change them for?

I could change **five** 5p coins for ☐ 1p coins.

b) I could change **seven** 5p coins for ☐ 1p coins.

c) I could change **nine** 5p coins for ☐ 1p coins.

d) I could change **eight** 5p coins for ☐ 1p coins.

3 **centimetres (cm)** or **metres (m)** or **kilometres (km)**?

a) I measure my calculator in _____ .

b) I measure the length of a room in _____ .

Review 7 • 115

4 You need
- squared paper.

a) Copy the journey below onto squared paper.

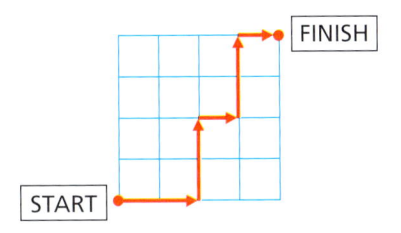

b) Write the moves and turns.
Use the codes **N**, **S**, **E**, **W** and **RT$\frac{1}{4}$** or **LT$\frac{1}{4}$**.

5 How much change from £20 if something cost:

a) £17? Change £☐

b) £12? Change £☐

c) £5? Change £☐

d) £9? Change £☐

e) £12? Change £☐

f) £14? Change £☐

8 Shape, space and measures

Estimating and measuring in mm, cm, m and km

Unit 8 words

kilometre (km)	height	width
further	millimetre (mm)	measure
length	about	remainder
metre (m)	more than	less than

Remember

Examples are shown in red.

means copy and complete.

You need
- a set of Unit 8 vocabulary Snap cards.

Play a game of Snap to help you learn the words.

Try the **word test** to get some points.

Estimating and measuring in mm, cm, m and km 117

metres (m) and kilometres (km)

1 My own **metre (m) reminder** is _____.

2 Measure a table in your classroom.

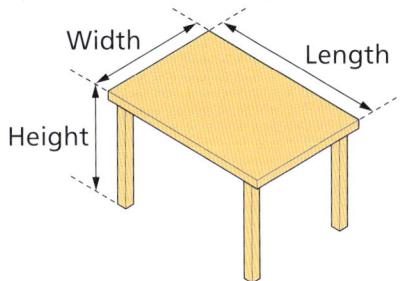

more than a metre or **less than** a metre or **about** a metre?

a) The **height** of the table is _____ a metre.

b) The **width** of the table is _____ a metre.

c) The **length** of the table is _____ a metre.

3 You need
- a metre rule
- chalk

One metre

a) Take the longest stride you can.
Get a partner to use a **metre** rule to see if your stride is

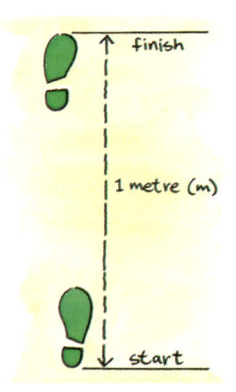

more than a metre or **less than** a metre or **about** a metre?

My stride is _____ a metre.

b) Copy the table below.
Use your **metre** strides to walk and chalk each distance.
Measure the distance you walked.
Tick the box to show if your walk was
more than or **less than** or **about right.**

	My distance is:		
Target distance	more than	less than	about right
2 metres (m)			
4 metres (m)			
8 metres (m)			
10 metres (m)			

4 If you started to walk from your school entrance,
what place do you think you would reach if you took:

a) 20 strides (about 20 m)

I think I would reach _____ .

Estimating and measuring in mm, cm, m and km **119**

b) 40 strides (about 40 m)

I think I would reach _____ .

c) 80 strides (about 80 m)

I think I would reach _____ .

d) 100 strides (about 100 m)

I think I would reach _____ .

e) Check the **100 m** out.
Take a **hundred strides** from the school entrance to see where you would really reach.

too short or **too long** or **about right**?

My guess was _____ .

f) You would walk a **long distance** if you walked **ten lots of 100 metres (m)**.
Talk to your partner about where you think you would reach.
Ask your teacher if your guess is about right.

5

Remember

We measure long distances in **kilometres** or **km** for short.

1000 metres (m) = 1 kilometre

This takes a lot of strides!

CITY CENTRE 3km ➡

There are ☐ **metres (m)** in **1 kilometre (km)**.

UNIT 8 SHAPE AND SPACE

6 See if you can go on a **relay walk**.
You need a group of **ten** people.

a) Each person takes a turn to walk and count **100 long strides**. The others walk normally.

b) When all ten have had a turn at counting 100 strides each, you have all walked about **one kilometre**.

7 Sue, Jo, Sanjay and Ben go to the same school.

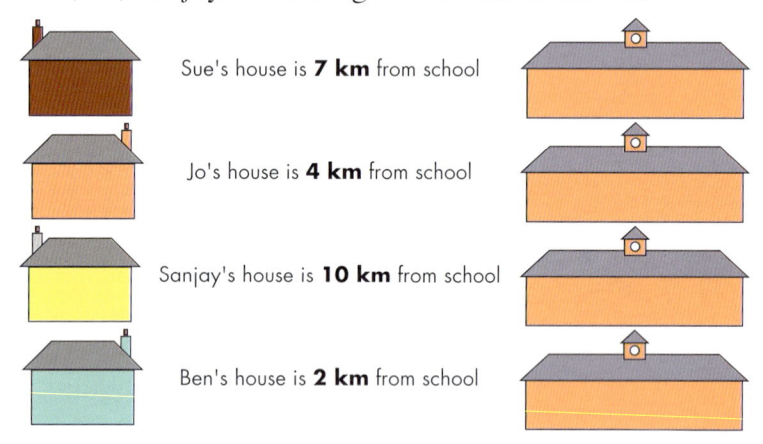

Sue's house is **7 km** from school

Jo's house is **4 km** from school

Sanjay's house is **10 km** from school

Ben's house is **2 km** from school

a) _____ lives **nearest** school.

b) _____ lives **furthest** away from school.

c) Sue lives ☐ km **nearer** school than Sanjay.

d) Sanjay lives ☐ km **further away** from school than Sue.

e) Ben lives ☐ km **nearer** school than Jo.

f) Jo lives ☐ km **further away** from school than Ben.

g) Jo lives ☐ times as far away from school as Ben.

Estimating and measuring in mm, cm, m and km • 121

centimetres (cm) and millimetres (mm)

8 My own **30 cm reminder** is _____ .

9 a) **Guess** the length of the lines **A–F** below.
Put the guesses in order – **shortest** length first.

b) You need
- a ruler which is marked in centimetres (cm).

Now **measure** the lines.

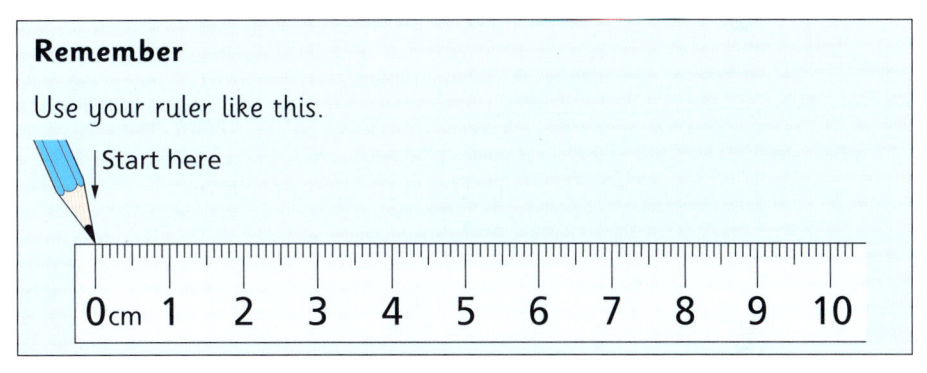

Remember

Use your ruler like this.

| Start here

0 cm 1 2 3 4 5 6 7 8 9 10

Put the **measured lengths** in order – **shortest** length first.

A ─────────────
B ──────────────────────
C ──────
D ────────────────────────────
E ─────────────────────
F ────

c) Line **D** is ☐ cm longer than line **E**.

d) A line 5 times as long as line **E** would measure ☐ cm.

e) Line **F** is ☐ cm shorter than line **B**.

f) A line 9 times as long as line **F** would measure ☐ cm.

g) A line twice as long as line **E** would measure ☐ cm.

h) A line half the length of line **E** would measure ☐ cm.

10 **About** how many **centimetres** are these measures? Round them **to the nearest 10 cm**.

52 cm is about 50 cm.

a) 48 cm is about ☐ cm.   b) 41 cm is about ☐ cm.

c) 45 cm is about ☐ cm.   d) 95 cm is about ☐ cm.

e) 97 cm is about ☐ cm.   f) 93 cm is about ☐ cm.

g) 52 cm is about ☐ cm.   h) 58 cm is about ☐ cm.

11 Name the shape:

square   rectangle   triangle   hexagon or **pentagon**?

Measure the sides.

a) hexagon – sides 2 cm, 2 cm, 2 cm, 2 cm, 2 cm, 2 cm

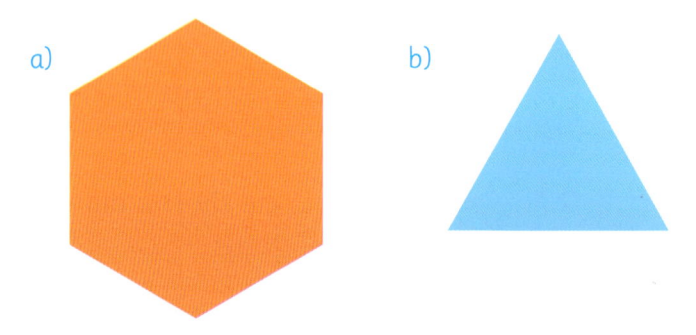

a)

b)

Estimating and measuring in mm, cm, m and km **123**

c)

d)

e)

f)

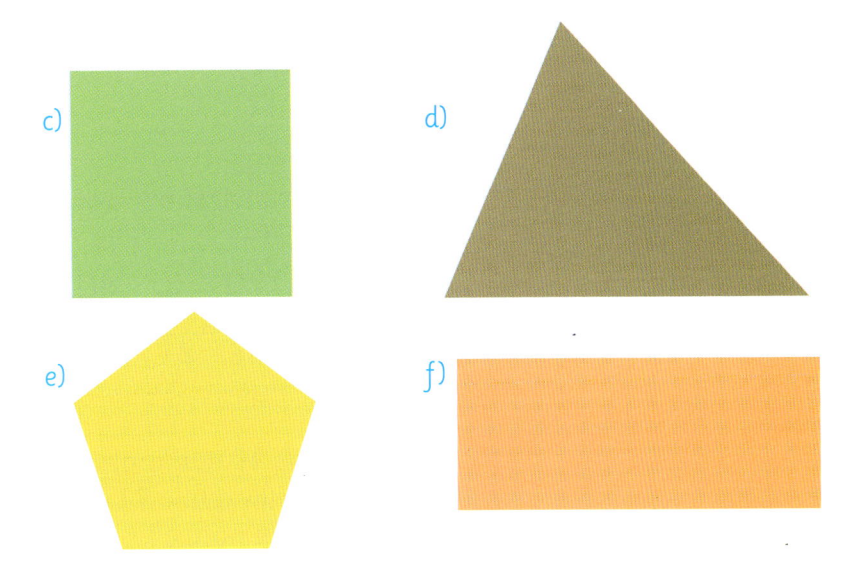

12 Try Worksheet 1 *Fit the shelf*.

13 We can measure very **small** things in **millimetres (mm)**.

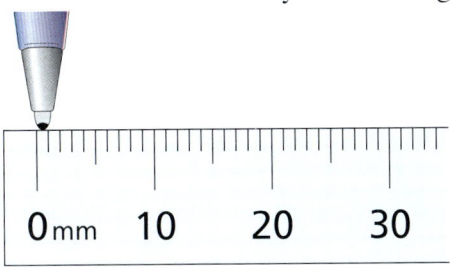

You need

- a ruler which is marked in millimetres (mm).

Find **three** things in your classroom which measure about

1 millimetre (mm).

Look at the **thickness** of things to help you.

14 Use Worksheet 2 to play a game of 'Snail's pace'.

124 UNIT 8 SHAPE AND SPACE

15 You need
- a ruler which shows **cm** and **mm**.

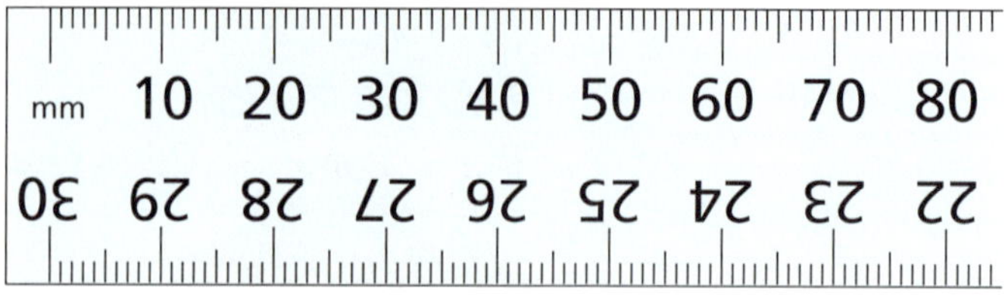

a) Draw a line **10 mm** long.
Below it draw a line **1 cm** long.
What do you notice?

b) Draw a line **100 mm** long.
Below it draw a line **10 cm** long.
What do you notice?

16 Use Worksheets 3 and 4 to play a game of 'Smiler'.

17 Fill in the missing measures:

| **metres (m)** | | **kilometres (km)** |
| **centimetres (cm)** | or | **millimetres (mm)** |

a) I measure a pin

in _____ .

b) I measure my waist

in _____ .

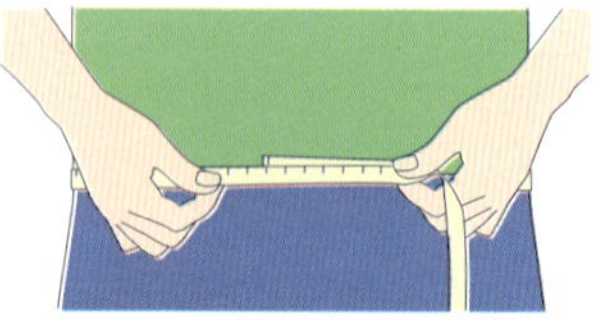

c) I measure a car

in _____ .

Estimating and measuring in mm, cm, m and km

d) I measure a road between towns

in _____ .

18 Play a game of 'Class guess'.

a) Someone holds up or points to an object or picture of an object.

b) Everyone writes down what they guess the **best measure** will be.

metres (m)   **kilometres (km)**
centimetres (cm)   or   **millimetres (mm)**

c) Two people collect the written guesses.

d) Your teacher says the correct measure.

e) Make a **table** like this. Choose a different object each day.

	Object	Correct	Incorrect
Monday	Book	15	16
Tuesday			
Wednesday			
Thursday			
Friday			

f) Take turns to keep a score of the number of correct answers each day.

g) Make a new table each week.

h) Which measure do most people get right?
Which measure do most people get wrong?
Are there more correct answers as the weeks go on?

Now try Unit 8 Test.

Review 8

1
a) 80p
  +20p
  ____

b) 56p
  +64p
  ____

c) 64p
  +70p
  ____

d) 37p
  +97p
  ____

e) 67p
  +68p
  ____

2 Choose:

very unlikely or **unlikely** or **likely** or **very likely**.

a) It is _____ that I will eat today.

b) It is _____ that I will fly an aeroplane today.

c) It is _____ that I will watch TV today.

d) It is _____ that I will walk 32 km today.

3 Write in order – **smallest** number first.

241   14   421   2401   41

4 How many 2p coins could I get from the following 1p coins?

Are there any 1p coins left over?

a) 12 1p coins

b) 13 1p coins

c) 16 1p coins

d) 17 1p coins

e) 11 (1p) coins   f) 14 (1p) coins

g) 20 (1p) coins   h) 1 (1p) coin

5 How many **more** square tiles and triangle tiles would be needed to fill this tiled wall?

6 a) 20p **take away** 4p   b) 20p − 10p

c) 17p **minus** 9p   d) 9p − 9p

e) 18p **subtract** 9p   f) 20p − 1p

g) 15p **minus** 5p   h) 10p − 10p

9 Number

Subtraction to 100

Unit 9 words

minus	between	more than
coins	large	amount
single	less than	left
digit	shape	half

Remember

Examples are shown in red.

means copy and complete.

You need
- a set of Unit 9 vocabulary Snap cards.

Play a game of Snap to help you learn the words.

Try the **word test** to get some points.

UNIT 9 NUMBER

> **Remember**
> You can **count on** to help you **take away**.
>
> 16 − 9 = ☐
>
> 9 and **how many more** makes 16?
> 9 and **7** makes 16.
> 16 − 9 = **7**

1   a) 16 − 9 = ☐   b) 17 − 8 = ☐   c) 16 − 8 = ☐   d) 15 − 6 = ☐

e) 13 − 7 = ☐   f) 12 − 5 = ☐   g) 11 − 9 = ☐   h) 10 − 7 = ☐

i) 10 − 10 = ☐   j) 10 − 0 = ☐

2   You need
- base 10 blocks.

Ann has a packet of biscuits.

She wants to eat **one single biscuit**.

She opens the packet.

She eats one.

She has these left.

She can show this **in figures**.

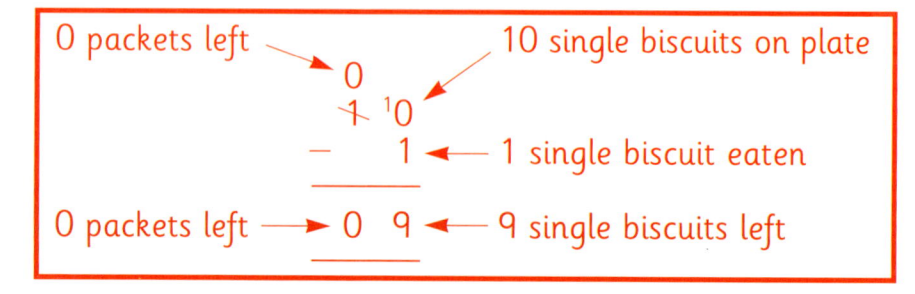

0 packets left ⟶ 0̶ ¹0   ⟵ 10 single biscuits on plate
   −   1   ⟵ 1 single biscuit eaten
0 packets left ⟶ 0 9   ⟵ 9 single biscuits left

Subtraction to 100

How many biscuits are left?

a) packets singles
```
  1 0
-   4
-----
```

b) packets singles
```
  1 0
-   6
-----
```

c) packets singles
```
  1 0
-   8
-----
```

d) packets singles
```
  1 0
-   5
-----
```

e) packets singles
```
  1 0
-   2
-----
```

f) packets singles
```
  1 0
-   3
-----
```

g) packets singles
```
  1 0
-   9
-----
```

h) packets singles
```
  1 0
-   1
-----
```

i) packets singles
```
  1 0
-   7
-----
```

j) packets singles
```
  1 0
-   0
-----
```

3 You **must** use
- base 10 blocks.

Nadia works in a supermarket at weekends.

UNIT 9 NUMBER

She has a packet of ten biscuits on the counter and six single biscuits on a plate for people to taste.

If the following biscuits were eaten, would she need to **open** the packet? Answer **Yes** or **No**.

a)

a) **No**

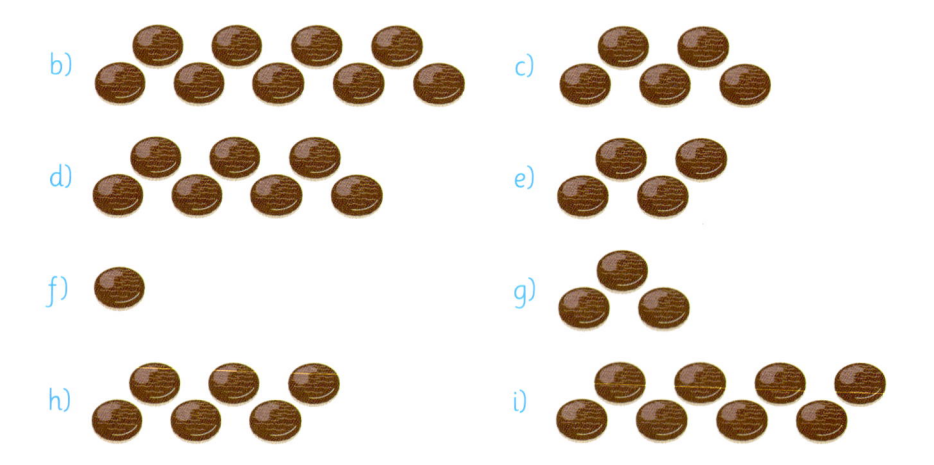

b)

c)

d)

e)

f)

g)

h)

i)

j) How many **packets** would she have left on the counter each time?

a) **1 packet left.**

4 Try Worksheet 1 *Have a taste (1)*.

5 You **must** use
- base 10 blocks.

How many biscuits are left?

Subtraction to 100 • 133

a) packets singles
      1 2
−   4
———

Set out your work to show where you have to open a packet.

0 packets left → 0
              1̶ ¹2 ← 12 single biscuits on plate
           −   4 ← 4 single biscuits eaten
             ———
0 packets left → 0 8 ← 8 single biscuits left

Remember

The **top line** shows **packets** and **single** biscuits on the counter **before** some biscuits were eaten.

a) packets singles b) packets singles c) packets singles
     1 2   1 5   1 6
 −   4   −   4   −   8

d) packets singles e) packets singles f) packets singles g) packets singles
     1 4   1 2   1 2   1 3
 −   5   −   2   −   6   −   9

h) packets singles i) packets singles j) packets singles
     1 9   1 7   1 8
 −   1   −   7   −   9

134 UNIT 9 NUMBER

6 You need
- 10p and 1p coins.

Mandy has 14p.
Will she need to change her 10p coin if she spends the following amounts?
Answer **Yes** or **No**.

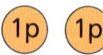

a) (1p)(1p)(1p)(1p)(1p)(1p)(1p)(1p)(1p)

a) Yes

b) (1p)(1p)(1p)(1p)(1p)   c) (1p)   d) (1p)(1p)(1p)(1p)(1p)(1p)(1p)(1p)

e) (1p)(1p)   f) (1p)(1p)(1p)(1p)   g) (1p)(1p)(1p)(1p)(1p)(1p)(1p)

h) (1p)(1p)(1p)   i) (1p)(1p)(1p)(1p)(1p)(1p)

j) How many 10p coins would she have left each time?
a) No 10p coins left.

7 Try Worksheet 2 *Change it (1)*.

8 You need
- 10p and 1p coins.

How much money is left?

a)   1 4p
  −   7p
  ―――

Subtraction to 100

Set out your work to show when the 10p coin has to be changed.

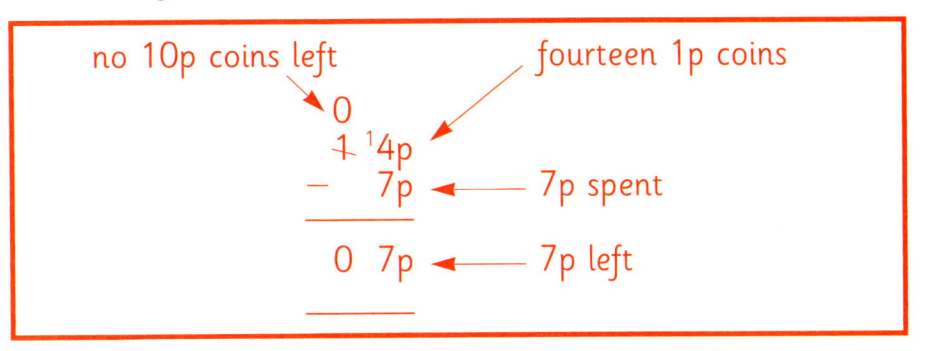

```
         no 10p coins left          fourteen 1p coins
                    ↘ 0
                     1̵ ¹4p ↙
                  −    7p    ← 7p spent
                    ─────
                     0  7p   ← 7p left
```

Remember

The **top line** shows the money **before** spending.

a) 1 4p
  − 7p

b) 1 8p
  − 4p

c) 1 6p
  − 9p

d) 1 7p
  − 8p

e) 1 5p
  − 2p

f) 1 2p
  − 5p

g) 1 5p
  − 9p

h) 1 9p
  − 9p

i) 1 3p
  − 6p

j) 1 6p
  − 8p

9 You **must** use
- base 10 blocks.

If Nadia had these biscuits on the counter

would she need to **open** a packet if the following single biscuits were eaten?
Answer **Yes** or **No**.

UNIT 9 NUMBER

a)

a) **Yes**

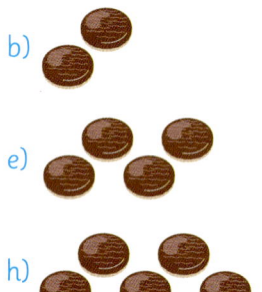

b)   c)   d)

e)   f)   g)

h)   i)   j)

?   k) How many **packets** would she have left on the counter each time?

a) 1 packet left.

10 Try Worksheet 3 *Have a taste (2)*.

11 How many biscuits are left?

a) packets singles
      2   2
   −   4
   ─────────

Set out your work to show when you have to open a packet.

> 1 packet of ten left   12 single biscuits on plate
>
>   1
>   2 ¹2
> −   4 ← 4 single biscuits eaten
> ─────────
>   1 8

Subtraction to 100 • 137

> **Remember**
> The **top line** shows packets and single biscuits on the counter **before** some biscuits were eaten.

a) packets singles
```
  2 2
-   4
-----
```

b) packets singles
```
  2 5
-   4
-----
```

c) packets singles
```
  2 6
-   8
-----
```

d) packets singles
```
  2 4
-   5
-----
```

e) packets singles
```
  2 2
-   2
-----
```

f) packets singles
```
  2 2
-   6
-----
```

g) packets singles
```
  2 3
-   9
-----
```

h) packets singles
```
  2 9
-   1
-----
```

i) packets singles
```
  2 7
-   7
-----
```

j) packets singles
```
  2 8
-   9
-----
```

12 Mandy has £27. Will she need to change a £10 note if she spends the following amounts? Answer **Yes** or **No**.

a) £12

a) No

b) £3   c) £0   d) £8

e) £5   f) £4   g) £1

h) £9   i) £6   j) £7

k) How many £10 notes would she have left each time?

a) One £10 note.

13 Try Worksheet 4 *Change it (2)*.

14 How much money is left?

a)
$$\begin{array}{r}£2\ 4\\-£\ \ \ 7\\\hline £\ \ \ \ \ \end{array}$$

Set out your work to show where you need to change a £10 note.

---

one £10 note left   fourteen £1 coins

$$\begin{array}{r}{}^{1}\\ \cancel{£2}\ \ {}^{1}4\\ -£\ \ \ 7\\\hline £1\ \ 7\end{array}$$

seven £1 coins spent

Remember

The **top line** shows money **before** spending.

Subtraction to 100 139

a) £2 4
 − £ 7
 £ ———

b) £2 8
 − £ 4
 £ ———

c) £2 6
 − £ 9
 £ ———

d) £2 7
 − £ 8
 £ ———

e) £2 5
 − £ 2
 £ ———

f) £2 2
 − £ 5
 £ ———

g) £2 5
 − £ 9
 £ ———

h) £2 9
 − £ 9
 £ ———

i) £2 3
 − £ 6
 £ ———

j) £2 6
 − £ 8
 £ ———

15 You may need
 • base 10 blocks.

If **eight** biscuits are eaten, how many **packets** would be left?

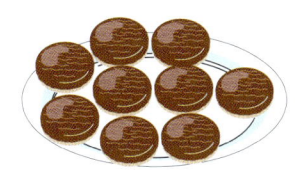

a)

a) 1 packet left.

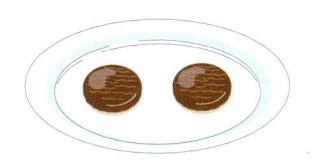

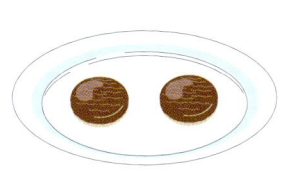

b)

c)

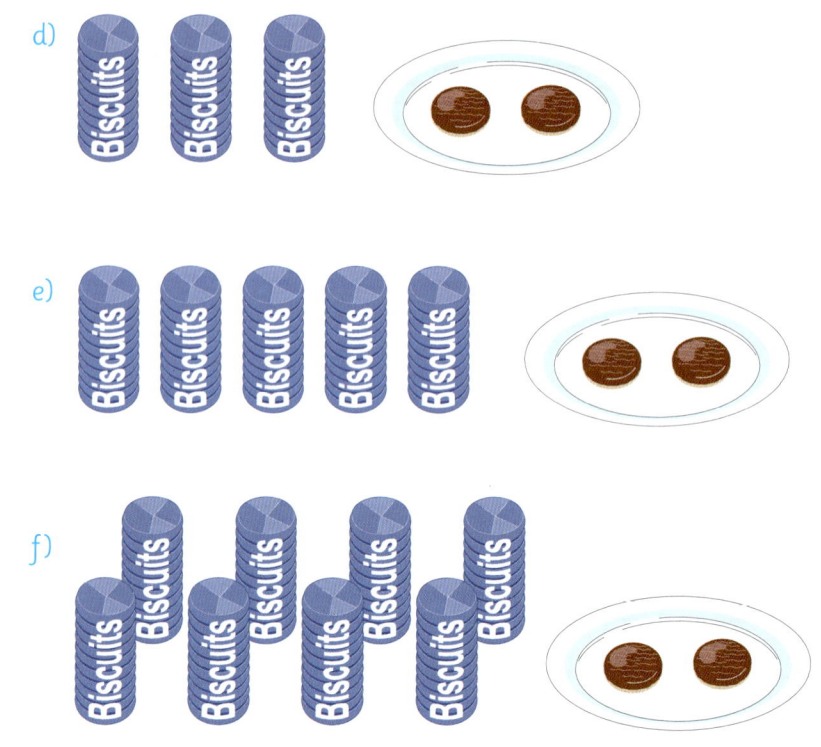

16 How many biscuits are left?

> **Remember**
>
> The **top line** shows packets and singles **before** some biscuits were eaten.

a) packets singles
```
    2   4
  –     0
  _____
```

b) packets singles
```
    2   4
  –     4
  _____
```

c) packets singles
```
    2   4
  –     8
  _____
```

d) packets singles
```
    6   3
  –     1
  _____
```

e) packets singles
```
    6   3
  –     8
  _____
```

f) packets singles
```
    8   2
  –     0
  _____
```

g) packets singles
```
    8   2
  –     2
  _____
```

h) packets singles
```
    8   2
  –     6
  _____
```

Subtraction to 100 • 141

i) packets   singles
```
   5  4
-     2
_____
```

j) packets   singles
```
   5  4
-     7
_____
```

k) packets   singles
```
   3  4
-     0
_____
```

l) packets   singles
```
   3  4
-     3
_____
```

m) packets   singles
```
   3  4
-     4
_____
```

n) packets   singles
```
   3  4
-     7
_____
```

o) packets   singles
```
   9  8
-     9
_____
```

17 Some people like the biscuits.
They buy some **packets**.
Nadia had these biscuits on the counter.

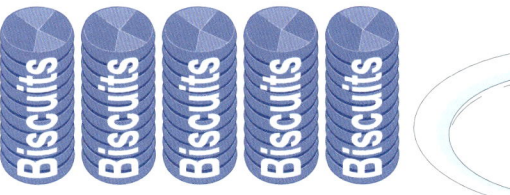

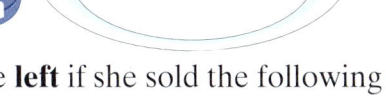

How many packets would be **left** if she sold the following number of **packets**?

a)
```
                packets  singles
                   5       0
packets sold → −   4       0
                _____
packets left →     1       0
```

b) packets   singles
```
   5  0
-  2  0
_____
```

c) packets   singles
```
   5  0
-  5  0
_____
```

d) packets   singles
```
   5  0
-  3  0
_____
```

e) packets   singles
```
   5  0
-  1  0
_____
```

18 Try Worksheet 5 *Sell a packet*.

19 Nadia had these biscuits on the counter.

How many biscuits would be **left** if some people ate **singles and** then bought **packets**?

```
              packets  singles
                 5       9
packets sold → − 1       2 ← singles eaten
              ─────────────
                 4       7
```

a) packets singles
```
    5  9
  − 1  2
  ──────
```

b) packets singles
```
    5  9
  − 2  3
  ──────
```

c) packets singles
```
    5  9
  − 1  1
  ──────
```

d) packets singles
```
    5  9
  − 3  4
  ──────
```

e) packets singles
```
    5  9
  − 4  6
  ──────
```

f) packets singles
```
    5  9
  − 5  5
  ──────
```

g) packets singles
```
    5  9
  − 3  7
  ──────
```

h) packets singles
```
    5  9
  − 2  5
  ──────
```

i) packets singles
```
    5  9
  − 4  8
  ──────
```

j) packets singles
```
    5  9
  − 2  9
  ──────
```

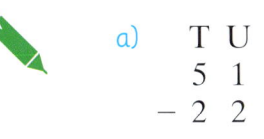

Subtraction to 100 • 143

20 How many left?

```
        T  U
        4
        5̶ ¹1
packets sold  − 2  2   singles tasted
        ─────
        2  9
```

a) T U   b) T U   c) T U   d) T U   e) T U
    5 1   4 0   3 5   3 5   7 4
  − 2 2   − 2 2   − 1 6   − 2 6   − 3 7
  ─────   ─────   ─────   ─────   ─────

f) T U   g) T U   h) T U   i) T U   j) T U
    7 0   8 4   8 0   4 8   4 0
  − 3 7   − 3 9   − 3 9   − 2 9   − 2 9
  ─────   ─────   ─────   ─────   ─────

21 Show where you change **1 ten** into **10 units**.

> **Remember**
>
> Always ask these **subtraction questions**:
>
> What number do I have at the start? See **top line**.
>
> Do I need to change a ten to take the units away?

a) T U   b) T U   c) T U   d) T U   e) T U
    9 5   1 8   5 7   8 0   7 0
  − 0 1   − 0 5   − 0 7   − 3 0   − 5 0
  ─────   ─────   ─────   ─────   ─────

144 UNIT 9 NUMBER

f) T U	g) T U	h) T U	i) T U	j) T U
8 9	1 2	1 2	3 4	5 4
− 8 5	− 6	− 0 5	− 9	− 0 7

k) T U	l) T U	m) T U	n) T U	o) T U
5 4	6 4	6 4	3 2	3 2
− 1 7	− 8	− 2 8	− 7	− 2 7

22 Some friends talk about the money they have saved for the holidays.

Tom £18 saved
Jan £46 saved
Jade £15 saved
Sarah £93 saved

a) Put the savings in order – **largest** amount first.

b) _____ has saved most money.

c) _____ has saved least money.

Subtraction to 100

Write down what Jan and Tom each saved.

d) Jan has saved £ ☐ **more than** Tom.

e) Tom has saved £ ☐ **less than** Jan.

f) The **difference between** Jan and Tom's savings is £ ☐.

Write down what Sarah and Jade each saved.

g) Sarah has saved £ ☐ **more than** Jade.

h) Jade has saved £ ☐ **less than** Sarah.

i) The **difference between** Jade and Sarah's savings is £ ☐.

Write down what Sarah and Tom each saved.

j) Sarah has saved £ ☐ **more than** Tom.

k) Tom has saved £ ☐ **less than** Sarah.

l) The **difference between** Tom and Sarah's savings is £ ☐.

m) All of the friends spent £9 each.
How much did each have left?

23 Try Worksheet 6 *Problem page*.

146 UNIT 9 NUMBER

24 These people are fed up.
They haven't saved a lot for the holidays.

I have only saved £5. — Joe

I have less money than Joe. I have saved £0. — Rashmi

I have less money than Rashmi. I have less than zero. — Sue

Is it possible to have **less than zero**?
Can you think of a reason why someone could have **less** than **zero**?
How could they show it in numbers?

25 Sue has **less than zero** because

I have less than zero, because I owe my sister £3. — Sue

Remember

We use the − sign to show numbers **less than 0**.

3 less than 0 is −3.

On the number line, the amounts of money in **Question 24** could be placed like this.

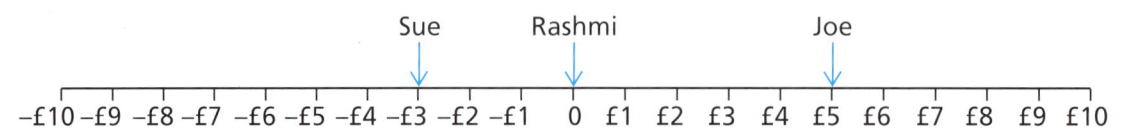

Sue ↓ at −£3   Rashmi ↓ at 0   Joe ↓ at £5

−£10 −£9 −£8 −£7 −£6 −£5 −£4 −£3 −£2 −£1 0 £1 £2 £3 £4 £5 £6 £7 £8 £9 £10

Subtraction to 100 • 147

Draw the number line above and arrow these people's savings to the line.

a) Ali has £8

b) Jill has £10

c) Ron owes £1

d) Mandy owes £8

26 Try Worksheets 7 and 8 *Savings line (1), (2)*.

27 You need
- a calculator.

Use your calculator to complete the following.

a) 2 − 0 = ☐   b) 2 − 1 = ☐   c) 2 − 2 = ☐   d) 2 − 3 = ☐

e) 3 − 1 = ☐   f) 3 − 2 = ☐   g) 3 − 3 = ☐   h) 3 − 4 = ☐

i) 4 − 2 = ☐   j) 4 − 3 = ☐   k) 4 − 4 = ☐   l) 4 − 5 = ☐

m) 5 − 3 = ☐   n) 5 − 4 = ☐   o) 5 − 5 = ☐   p) 5 − 6 = ☐

Write down any other subtraction which will give an answer of: ☐ − 1

28 You need
- Unit 9 Race against time cards
- your 'My maths record' sheet.

Race against time

1 Sort the race cards – this side up.

	T	U
	1	8
−		9

2 Take the cards **one** at a time.

3 Do you need to change a ten,
Yes or No?
Answer as quickly as you can.

4 Did you get it right?
Look at the other side of the card.

Yes

5 When you get all the answers correct, ask a friend to test you.

6 Now **Race against time**.

Go for points!

Ask your teacher to test and time you.

Remember

3 errors – 1 point

2 errors – 2 points

1 error – 3 points

0 errors – 5 points

Answer in 1 minute with 0 errors – 7 points

Now try Unit 9 Test.

Review 9

1
a) 83p
  + 28p
  ─────

b) 92p
  − 39p
  ─────

c) 57p
  + 67p
  ─────

d) 64p
  + 38p
  ─────

e) 62p
  − 18p
  ─────

2
a) 10 × 5 = ☐

b) 7 × 5 = ☐

c) 9 × 5 = ☐

d) 5 × 5 = ☐

e) 4 × 5 = ☐

f) 6 × 5 = ☐

g) 2 × 5 = ☐

h) 1 × 5 = ☐

i) 3 × 5 = ☐

j) 8 × 10 = ☐

3 Pick the **measures** used for **length**, **weight** or **liquid** volume.

centimetre (**cm**)   gram (**g**)   millimetre (**mm**)
half litre ($\frac{1}{2}$ **l**)   litre (**l**)   kilometre (**km**)
kilogram (**kg**)   metre (**m**)

a) The **length** measures are _____ .

150 UNIT 9 NUMBER

b) The **weight** measures are _____ .

c) The **liquid** measures are _____ .

4 Pick the **measuring tool** used to find **length**, **weight** or **liquid volume**.

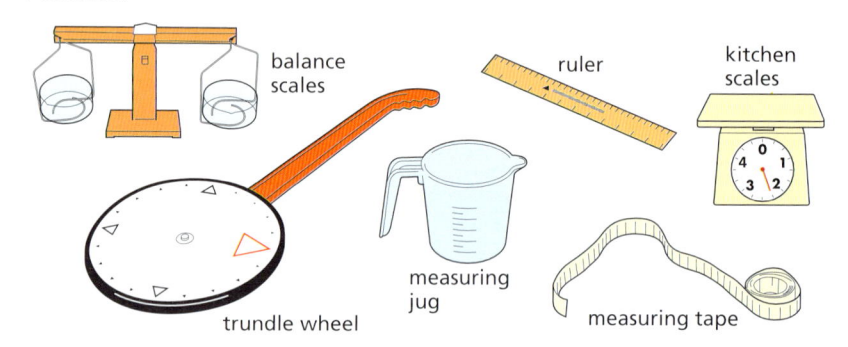

balance scales
ruler
kitchen scales
trundle wheel
measuring jug
measuring tape

a) The **length** measuring tools are _____ .

b) The **weight** measuring tools are _____ .

c) The **liquid volume** measuring tools are _____ .

5 Write these times in **two** ways: minutes **past** the hour **and** either **quarter past** or **quarter to**.

a) It is ☐ minutes past 4.

It is a _____ 5.

b) It is ☐ minutes past 4.

It is a _____ 4.

10 Measures

Weight and capacity: g, kg, ml and l

Unit 10 words

weight	balance	litre (l)
millilitre (ml)	weigh	heaviest
lightest	gram (g)	kilogram (kg)
centimetre (cm)	liquid	scale

Remember

Examples are shown in red.

means copy and complete.

You need
- a set of Unit 10 vocabulary Snap cards.

Play a game of Snap to help you learn the words.

Try the **word test** to get some points.

UNIT 10 MEASURES

A Weight

Remember

kg stands for **k**ilo**g**ram

bag of sugar   packet of cornflakes

1 a) A _____ weighs 1 kg.

b) A _____ weighs half a kilogram.

Remember

½ kg = 500 g

c) We write _____ as short for kilogram.

d) We can write half a kilogram as ☐ kg or ☐ g.

2   You need

- one of each of these coins –

- a set of balance scales

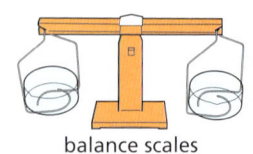

balance scales

- a calculator

Weight and capacity: g, kg, ml and l

We weigh light objects in **grams**.

weighs about **1 gram**.

Remember

g stands for **gram**.

a) Copy and complete the table below.

Coin	Weight
1p	
2p	
5p	
10p	
20p	
50p	
£1	

b) The ☐ coin is lightest.

c) The ☐ coin is heaviest.

d) Altogether the coins weigh ☐ g.

e) How many ways can you make different coins balance? Write them down.

(2p) (2p) weighs the same as (£1).

You can use mixtures of coins to get a balance.

UNIT 10 MEASURES

f) Ali has 55 g of 10p coins.

Sue has 34 g of £1 coins.

Who has most money?
Tell your teacher how you worked it out.

3 a) What is the heaviest weight you could get on these scales?

If you use a magnifying glass you would see that you count on in 5s to read the scale.

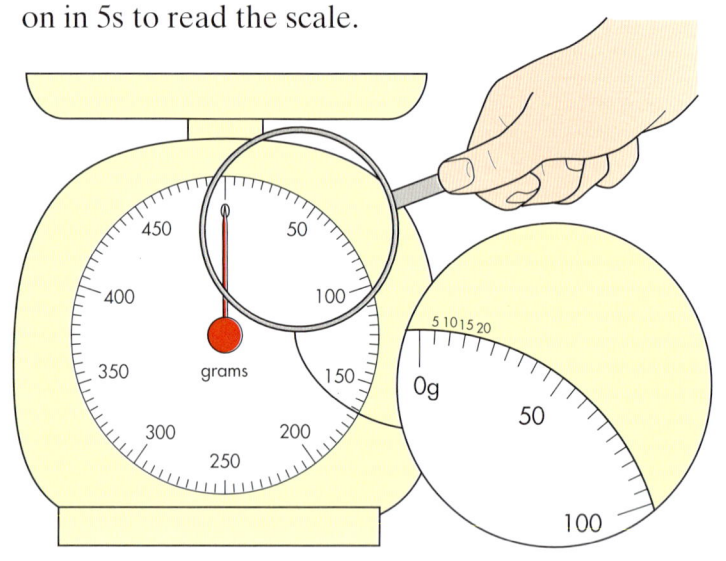

Fill in the missing numbers on these scales.

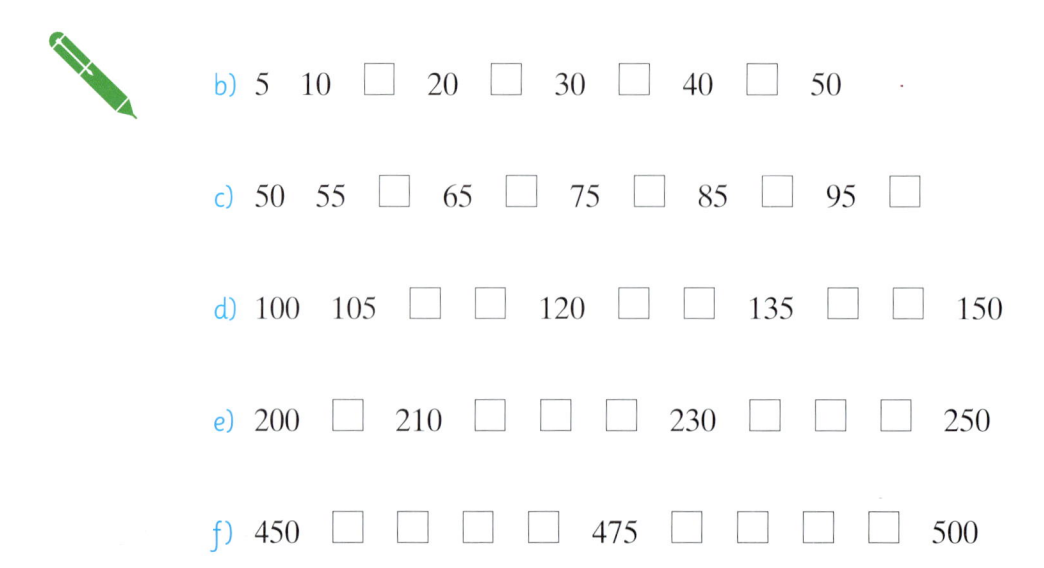

b) 5 10 ☐ 20 ☐ 30 ☐ 40 ☐ 50

c) 50 55 ☐ 65 ☐ 75 ☐ 85 ☐ 95 ☐

d) 100 105 ☐ ☐ 120 ☐ ☐ 135 ☐ ☐ 150

e) 200 ☐ 210 ☐ ☐ ☐ 230 ☐ ☐ ☐ 250

f) 450 ☐ ☐ ☐ ☐ 475 ☐ ☐ ☐ ☐ 500

Weight and capacity: g, kg, ml and l • 155

4 Try Worksheets 1 and 2 *Read the scale in 5s (1), (2)*.

5 a) What is the heaviest weight you could get on these scales? If you use a magnifying glass you would see that you count on in 10s to read the scale.

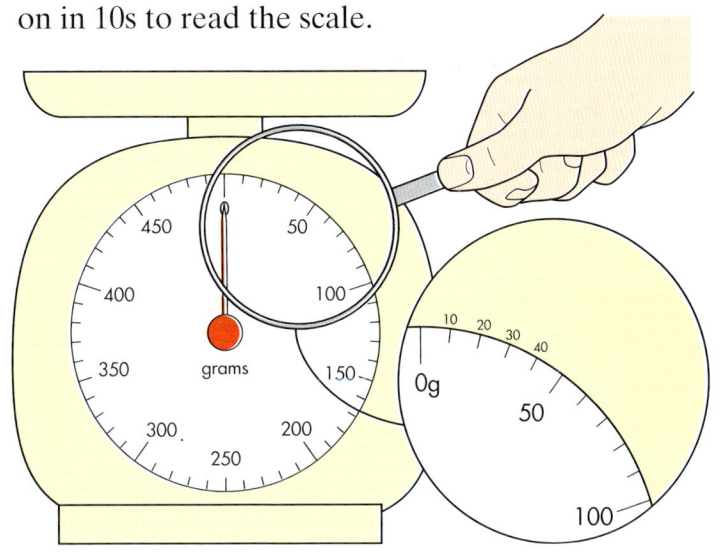

Fill in the missing numbers on these scales.

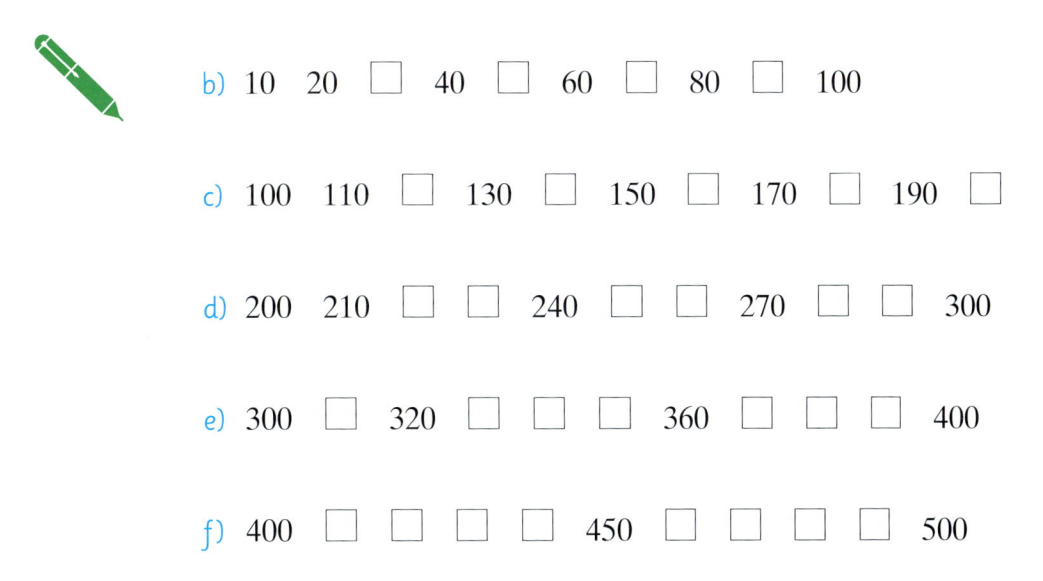

b) 10 20 ☐ 40 ☐ 60 ☐ 80 ☐ 100

c) 100 110 ☐ 130 ☐ 150 ☐ 170 ☐ 190 ☐

d) 200 210 ☐ ☐ 240 ☐ ☐ 270 ☐ ☐ 300

e) 300 ☐ 320 ☐ ☐ ☐ 360 ☐ ☐ ☐ 400

f) 400 ☐ ☐ ☐ ☐ 450 ☐ ☐ ☐ ☐ 500

6 Try Worksheets 3 and 4 *Read the scale in 10s (1), (2)*.

156 UNIT 10 MEASURES

7 Do you count on in 5s or 10s to read these scales?

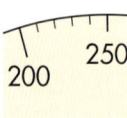

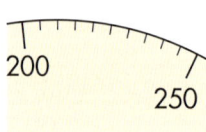

Scale A: 200, 250

Scale B: 200, 250

a) In scale **A** you count on in ☐.

b) In scale **B** you count on in ☐.

8 Try Worksheet 5 *Which scale?*

9 You may need
- a set of balance scales and weights.

How many different ways can you balance $\frac{1}{2}$ kg (500 g)? Write them down.

50 × 10g = 1 × 500g

10 a) 1 whole = ☐ halves

b) $\frac{1}{2}$ kg = ☐ g

c) You may need
- a set of balance scales and weights.

1 kg = ☐ g

Weight and capacity: g, kg, ml and l 157

11 Are these weights **more** or **less** than 1 kg?

> **Remember**
> 1 kg = 1000 g

a) 500 g are **less** than 1 kg.

b) 1500 g are _____ than 1 kg.

c) 1800 g are _____ than 1 kg.

d) 800 g are _____ than 1 kg.

e) 20 g are _____ than 1 kg.

f) 200 g are _____ than 1 kg.

g) 999 g are _____ than 1 kg.

h) 1001 g are _____ than 1 kg.

12 Try Worksheet 6 *More or less than a kilogram?*

13 You may need
- a set of balance scales and weights.

How many different ways can you balance 1 kg? Write them down.

2 × 500g = 1 × 1kg

UNIT 10 MEASURES

14 You may need
- a calculator.

These people carry home their shopping.

Lin's bag: Jam 450 g, Salt 750 g, Coffee 300 g

Ben's bag: Beans 400 g, Bisto 227 g, Pepper 25 g

Sal's bag: Biscuits 340 g, Coffee 300 g, Butter 500 g

more than or **less** than 1 kg?

a) Lin's bag is _____ than 1 kg.

b) Ben's bag is _____ than 1 kg.

c) Sal's bag is _____ than 1 kg.

d) Who has the **heaviest** bag?

e) Who has the **lightest** bag?

15 Put these weights in order – **smallest** weight first.

20 g   2 kg   1000 g $\frac{1}{2}$ kg   1020 g   20 kg

Weight and capacity: g, kg, ml and l • 159

16 Which **measure** would you use:

grams (g) or kilograms (kg)?

a) I weigh a coin in _____ .

b) I weigh flour in _____ .

c) I weigh potatoes in _____ .

d) I weigh myself in _____ .

Class guess

17 Play a game of 'Class guess' each day for a week.

> **Rules for 'Class guess'**
>
> 1 An object is passed around the room.
>
> 2 Everyone writes down whether they think the object is
>   - less than half a kilogram
>   - more than half a kilogram or
>   - more than a kilogram
>
> 3 Two people collect the written guesses.
>
> 4 Weigh the object.
>
> 5 Keep score of the correct guesses.
>
>   Monday – **6** correct guesses.
>
> 6 At the end of the week, draw a **block graph**.
>
>   Put 5 columns along the bottom, for Monday to Friday.
>
>   Put the numbers for correct guesses up the side.

B Liquid measure

> **Remember**
>
> **l** stands for **l**itre.

1

a) A bottle of _____ holds a **litre**.

b) A bottle of _____ holds about **half a litre**.

c) My own **litre** reminder is _____ .

d) My own **half litre** reminder is _____ .

2   0 10 20 30 40 50 ☐ ☐ ☐ ☐ ☐

    0 20 40 60 80 100 ☐ ☐ ☐ ☐ ☐

    0 50 100 150 200 250 ☐ ☐ ☐ ☐ ☐

3 Kevin and Sal bake a cake for their sister's birthday. They measure smaller amounts of liquid in **m**illi**l**itres.

> **Remember**
>
> **ml** stands for **m**illi**l**itres.
>
> **500 m**illi**l**itres = $\frac{1}{2}$ litre

Weight and capacity: g, kg, ml and l • **161**

This is the measuring jug they used.

If you look at the bottom of the scale you will see this.

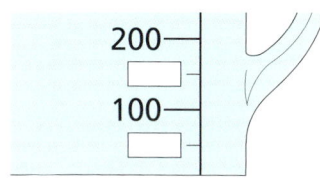

? What numbers do you think the shorter marks stand for?

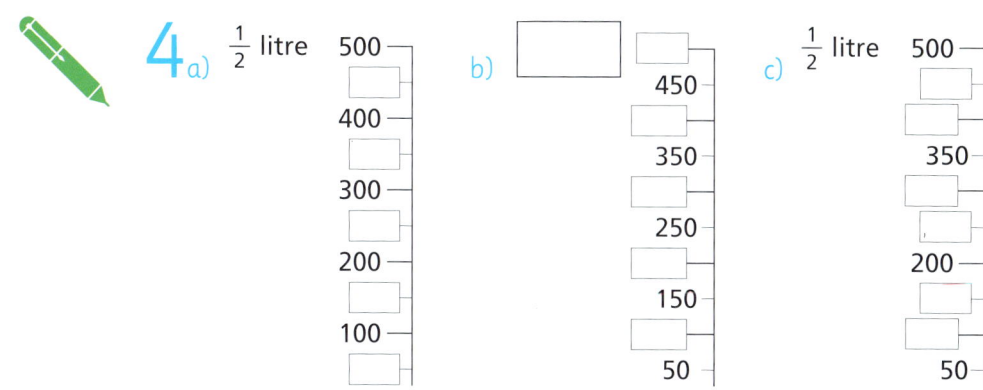

4 a) ½ litre 500, 400, 300, 200, 100

b) 450, 350, 250, 150, 50

c) ½ litre 500, 350, 200, 50

5 a) What is the largest amount you could measure in the jug on page 161?

b) What would you do if you wanted to measure a **litre** or **1½ litres**?

c) Where would a ¼ **litre** be written on the scale?

6 a) 1 whole = ☐ halves

b) ½ l = ☐ ml

c) You may need
- a litre measure.

1 l = ☐ ml

7 Are these amounts **more** or **less** than 1 l?

> **Remember**
> **1000** ml = **1 l**

a) 500 ml are **less** than 1 l.

b) 1500 ml are _____ than 1 l.

c) 1800 ml are _____ than 1 l.

Weight and capacity: g, kg, ml and l 163

d) 800 ml are _____ than 1 l.

e) 20 ml are _____ than 1 l.

f) 200 ml are _____ than 1 l.

g) 999 ml are _____ than 1 l.

h) 1001 ml are _____ than 1 l.

8 Try Worksheet 7 *More or less than a litre?*

9 Put these amounts of liquid in order – **smallest** first.

20 ml   2 ml   1000 ml $\frac{1}{2}$ l   1020 ml   1500 ml

10 Can you write these amounts of liquid in a different way?

a) 1000 ml   b) 500 ml   c) 1500 ml

11 Which **measure** would you use:
millilitres (ml) or **litres (l)**?

a) I measure water for a baby's bath in _____ .

b) I measure water to make a cake in _____ .

UNIT 10 MEASURES

12 Match the **measuring tool** to the job.

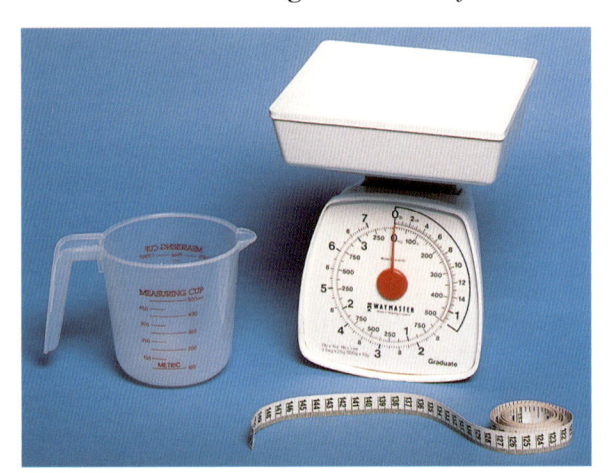

a) I measure my waist with a _____ .

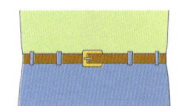

b) I measure butter to put in a cake with a _____ .

c) I measure water to make jelly with a _____ .

13 Try Worksheet Puzzle *Cold drinks*.

Now try Unit 10 Test.

Review 10

1 a) 1 0p
  +   5p
  ─────

b) 1 0p
  −   5p
  ─────

c) 1 7p
  +   5p
  ─────

d) 1 8p
  −   9p
  ─────

e) 3 4p
  + 2 5p
  ─────

2 You need
- squared paper.

Look carefully at each scale.
Copy it onto squared paper.
Shade the **bars** to show:

a) 8 people
b) 30 people
c) 9 people
d) 35 people
e) 17 people

3 Draw the people. 👤 = 10 people

a)   = 50 people

b)   = 35 people

4 Write the **value** of the 3 – **thousands**, **hundreds**, **tens** or **units**.

a) 1 2 5 ③   b) ③ 1 0 9

c) ③ 4 1   d) 1 0 ③ 4

5 a) 5 × 4 = ☐   b) 7 × 5 = ☐

c) 9 × 2 = ☐   d) 9 × 5 = ☐

e) 4 × 3 = ☐

6 a) 10 ÷ 2   b) 11 ÷ 2

c) 30 ÷ 10   d) 39 ÷ 10

e) 100 ÷ 10

7 Name **two** things you measure in

a) litres (l)   b) kilograms (kg)

c) metres (m)

8 Write these measures – to the **nearest 10**.

a) 83 cm   b) 283 cm   c) 59 g

d) 459 g   e) 35 ml   f) 235 ml

9 100 ☐ 120 ☐ 140 ☐ 160 ☐ 180

11 Number

Division by 2, 3, 4, 5 and 10

Unit 11 words

share	left over	longest
shortest	day	week
different	coins	each
between	divide	remainder

Remember

Examples are shown in red.

✎ means copy and complete.

You need
- a set of Unit 11 vocabulary Snap cards.

Play a game of Snap to help you learn the words.

Try the **word test** to get some points.

1 5 10 15 20 ☐ ☐ ☐ ☐ ☐ ☐

2 Five friends share 50 buns equally.

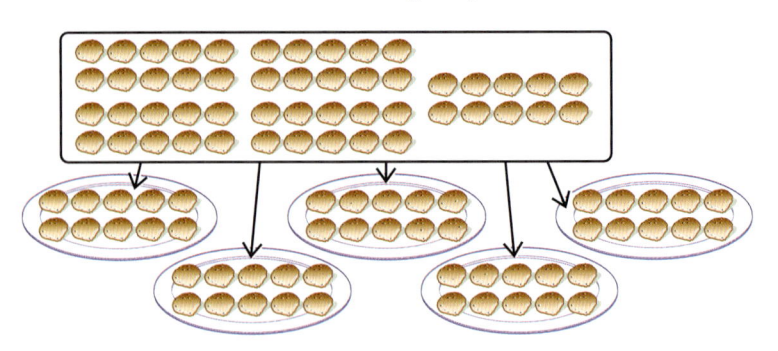

They get 10 buns each.
50 buns **shared between 5** is **10** buns.
Share these buns equally.

a) 50 buns shared between 5 is ☐ buns.   50 ÷ 5 = ☐

b) 10 buns shared between 5 is ☐ buns.   10 ÷ 5 = ☐

c) 15 buns shared between 5 is ☐ buns.   15 ÷ 5 = ☐

d) 20 buns shared between 5 is ☐ buns.   20 ÷ 5 = ☐

3 Try Worksheet 1 *Five shares*.

4 How many jumps of 5 to reach 35?

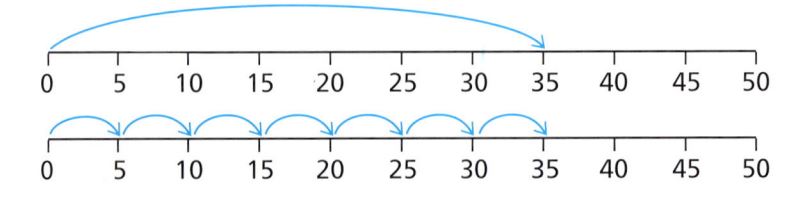

It takes **7** jumps of **5** to reach **35**.

Division by 2, 3, 4, 5 and 10 • 169

a) It takes ☐ jumps of 5 to reach **30**.

b) It takes ☐ jumps of 5 to reach **25**.

c) It takes ☐ jumps of 5 to reach **20**.

5 Try Worksheets 2 and 3 *Jumping fives (1), (2)*.

6 Here are different ways of showing **20 ÷ 5**.

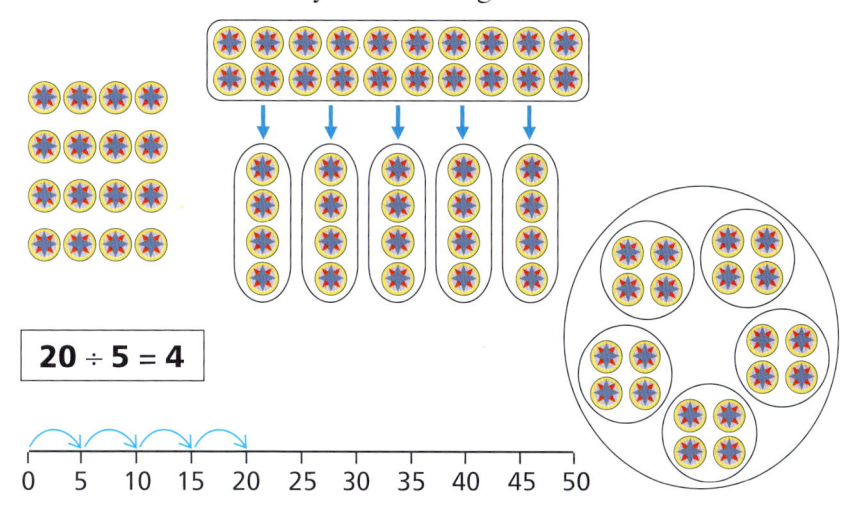

$20 \div 5 = 4$

Make your own chart for **15 ÷ 5**

7 If we share 21 sweets between 5 people

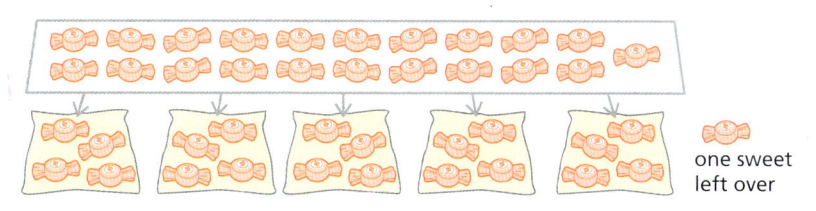

one sweet left over

each person will get **4 sweets**.
There will be **1 sweet** left over.

UNIT 11 NUMBER

	Each	Left over
20 sweets ÷ 5	4 sweets	0
21 sweets ÷ 5		
22 sweets ÷ 5		
10 sweets ÷ 5		
11 sweets ÷ 5		
12 sweets ÷ 5		
15 sweets ÷ 5		
16 sweets ÷ 5		
17 sweets ÷ 5		

8 Try Worksheet 4 *Left overs (1)*.

9 Lin packs pens in boxes of **five**.

a) She puts 10 pens in **2** boxes with **0** pens left over.

b) She puts 11 pens in **2** boxes with **1** left over.

Division by 2, 3, 4, 5 and 10

c) She puts 14 pens in ☐ boxes with ☐ pens left over.

d) She puts 20 pens in ☐ boxes with ☐ pens left over.

e) She puts 22 pens in ☐ boxes with ☐ pens left over.

f) She puts 30 pens in ☐ boxes with ☐ pens left over.

g) She puts 34 pens in ☐ boxes with ☐ pens left over.

h) She puts 45 pens in ☐ boxes with ☐ pens left over.

i) She puts 49 pens in ☐ boxes with ☐ pens left over.

10 You need
- a box of coins.

For work experience Jane counts (1p) coins in a shop.

She will then take them to the bank to get (5p) coins instead.

UNIT 11 NUMBER

How many stacks of 5 can Jane make from these numbers of 1p coins?

a) 10 (1p) coins make ☐ stacks of 5.

b) 20 (1p) coins make ☐ stacks of 5.

c) 30 (1p) coins make ☐ stacks of 5.

d) 45 (1p) coins make ☐ stacks of 5.

e) 15 (1p) coins make ☐ stacks of 5.

f) 5 (1p) coins make ☐ stacks of 5.

g) 25 (1p) coins make ☐ stacks of 5.

h) 35 (1p) coins make ☐ stacks of 5.

i) 40 (1p) coins make ☐ stacks of 5.

j) 50 (1p) coins make ☐ stacks of 5.

Division by 2, 3, 4, 5 and 10 • 173

11 Change the following amounts into 5p coins.

Show where there are 1p coins left over.

a) 12p

a) 12p ÷ 5 = 2 5p coins and 2 1p coins left over

12 ÷ 5 = 2 remainder 2

b) 22p c) 30p d) 32p

e) 40p f) 42p g) 25p

h) 27p i) 45p j) 48p

12 a) Which of these amounts could you pay using **only 2p** coins?

4p   7p   8p   23p   47p

You could pay the ☐p and the ☐p.

b) Which of these amounts could you pay using **only £10 notes**?

£25   £40   £81   £100   £1

You could pay the £☐ and the £☐.

c) Which of these amounts could you pay using **only £5 notes**?

£12   £40   £43   £38   £5

You could pay the £☐ and the £☐.

UNIT 11 NUMBER

13 Try Worksheet 5 *Number machines (1)*.

14 Try Worksheet Puzzle *Place the chairs*.

15 a) 2 ☐ 6 ☐ 10 ☐ 14 ☐ 18 ☐

b) 10 ☐ 30 ☐ 50 ☐ 70 ☐ 90 ☐

c) 5 ☐ 15 ☐ 25 ☐ 35 ☐ 45 ☐

d) 3 ☐ 9 ☐ 15 ☐ 21 ☐ 27 ☐

16 Try Worksheet 6 *Jumping threes*.

17 You need
- a group of 12 people.

Put the following numbers of people into **three equal groups**:

a) 12 people
There are ☐ people in each group.

b) 6 people
There are ☐ people in each group.

c) 9 people
There are ☐ people in each group.

Now put the following numbers of people into **groups of three**:

d) 12 people
There are ☐ groups of three.

Division by 2, 3, 4, 5 and 10

e) 6 people
There are ☐ groups of three.

f) 9 people
There are ☐ groups of three.

What do you notice about the answers?

18 Try Worksheet 7 *Left overs (2)*.

19

Remember
Write down the **remainders** where there are any.
You can write **r** as short for **remainder**.

a) $10 \div 2 =$ ☐   b) $11 \div 2 =$ ☐   c) $14 \div 2 =$ ☐

d) $15 \div 2 =$ ☐   e) $15 \div 5 =$ ☐   f) $17 \div 5 =$ ☐   g) $25 \div 5 =$ ☐

h) $28 \div 5 =$ ☐   i) $35 \div 5 =$ ☐   j) $39 \div 5 =$ ☐   k) $40 \div 10 =$ ☐

l) $46 \div 10 =$ ☐   m) $20 \div 10 =$ ☐   n) $24 \div 10 =$ ☐   o) $58 \div 10 =$ ☐

20 Jo saw these things in a catalogue.
He ordered some things for himself and his brother.

J50 Jacket
T30 T-shirt
S20 Socks
B40 Belt

This is his order form.
Copy the table and fill in the Number wanted.

Order form				
Code	Item	Cost for 1	Total cost	Number wanted
J50	jacket	£10	£20	
B40	belt	£3	£12	
T30	t-shirt	£5	£15	
S20	socks	£2 (pair)	£12	(pairs)

21 Find the answers to the sums.
Each answer stands for a letter below.
Write the letters and read the words they make.

D	E	L	N	O	W
5	7	4	3	2	6

$60 \div 10 = \square$ $35 \div 5 = \square$ $20 \div 5 = \square$ $12 \div 3 = \square$
W

$50 \div 10 = \square$ $20 \div 10 = \square$ $9 \div 3 = \square$ $70 \div 10 = \square$

22 Try Worksheet 8 *Number machines (2)*.

23 You need
- Unit 11 Race against time cards
- Unit 5 Race against time cards
- your 'My maths record' sheet.

Division by 2, 3, 4, 5 and 10

Race against time

1 Sort the Unit 11 Race cards – this side up.

$20 \div 5$

2 Take the cards one at a time.

3 Answer as quickly as you can.

4 Did you get it right? Look at the other side of the card.

4

5 When you get all the answers correct, ask a friend to test you.

6 Now **Race against time**.

Go for points!

Ask your teacher to test and time you.

7 Now try the Unit 5 Race cards – this side up.

4×5

8 You can go for more points.

Remember

3 errors – 1 point

2 errors – 2 points

1 error – 3 points

0 errors – 5 points

Answer in 1 minute with 0 errors – 7 points

Now try Unit 11 Test.

Review 11

1
a) 4 8p
  − 1 4p
  _____

b) 5 2p
  −   4p
  _____

c) 4 8p
  + 5 8p
  _____

d) 8 0p
  − 1 1p
  _____

e) 2 7p
  + 1 9p
  _____

2 Are these **measures** for **length** or measures for **weight**?

a) centimetre (cm) _____   b) millimetre (mm) _____

c) gram (g) _____   d) metre (m) _____

e) kilogram (kg) _____   f) kilometre (km) _____

3 Fill in a.m. or p.m.

a) (during the night) 2.00 _._.   b) breakfast 9.00 _._.

c) evening 7.00 _._.

4 Fill in the missing compass points.

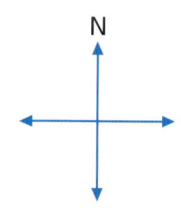

N

5 Write the next decimal number going **up** the scale.

a) 0.9 → ☐.☐   b) 1.0 → ☐.☐   c) 1.9 → ☐.☐

6 Write the next decimal number going **down** the scale.

a) 0.2 → ☐.☐   b) 3.0 → ☐.☐   c) 5.1 → ☐.☐

7 km (kilometres), m (metres), cm (centimetres) or mm (millimetres)?

a) I measure the length of the room in _____ .

b) I measure the distance from one town to another in _____ .

c) I measure the thickness of a coin in _____ .

d) I measure the length of my book in _____ .

8 Write in order – **smallest** number first.

30   3   3.5   350   5.3   5

12 Measures

Time: 24-hour clock and calendars

Unit 12 words

month	calendar	date
before	after	timetable
time	minute	second
hour	longest	shortest

Remember

Examples are shown in red

means copy and complete.

You need
- a set of Unit 12 vocabulary Snap cards.

Play a game of Snap to help you learn the words.

Try the **word test** to get some points.

1 Put these periods of time in order – shortest period of time first.

a) $\frac{1}{2}$ hour　　　　　　　　b) 60 minutes

Time: 24-hour clock and calendars

c) a quarter of an hour

d) 45 minutes

e) two hours

f) a day

2 Put these times in order – **earliest** time first.

a) [clock showing time]

b) quarter past six

c) 11 : 45

d) 2 : 30

e) [clock showing time]

f) ¼ to eleven

3 Try Worksheet 1 *Set it right*.

4 Fill in **minutes** or **hours**.

a) The **small** hand on the clock shows the _____ .

b) The **large** hand on the clock shows the _____ .

c) How many times does the **large** hand go round in **1 day**?

d) How many times does the **small** hand go around in **1 day**?

UNIT 12 MEASURES

5 You need
- a clock face with movable hands.

Look at the **small** hand on each of these clock faces.

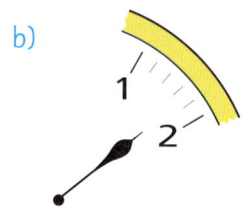

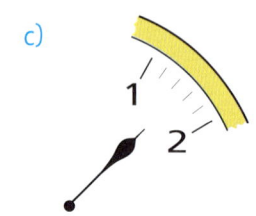

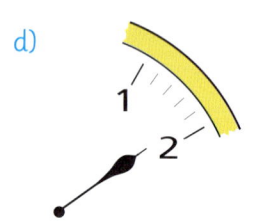

a)

b)

c)

d)

Talk to your partner about where you think the missing **large hand** would be on each clock face.

How many **minutes** has the large hand gone from the **last** hour?
How many **minutes** has it still to go to the **next** hour?

Remember
The large (minute) hand travels **60 minutes** in **1 hour**.

Time: 24-hour clock and calendars • 183

6 On this side of the clock we can say the time in **different ways**. What other way can we say these times?

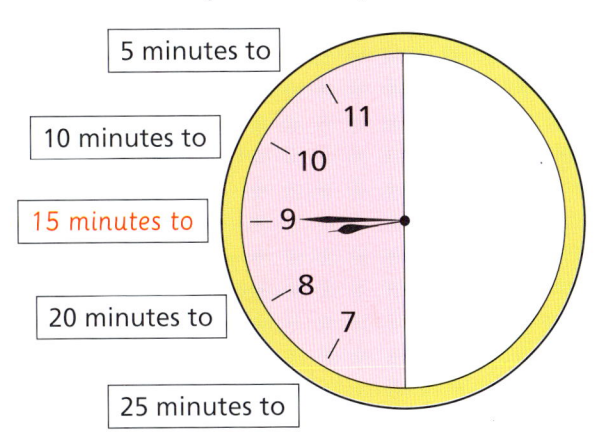

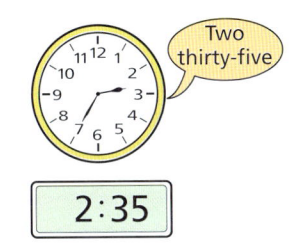

- 5 minutes to
- 10 minutes to
- 15 minutes to
- 20 minutes to
- 25 minutes to

Two thirty-five — 2:35

a) The time is _____ to _____ .

Two forty — 2:40

b) The time is _____ to _____ .

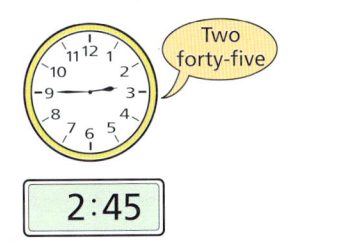

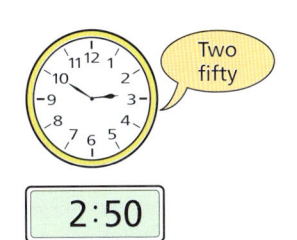

Two forty-five — 2:45

c) The time is _____ to _____ .

Two fifty — 2:50

d) The time is _____ to _____ .

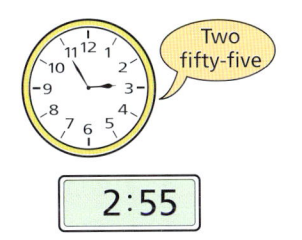

Two fifty-five — 2:55

e) The time is _____ to _____ .

184 UNIT 12 MEASURES

7 Try Worksheets 2 and 3 *Different ways (1), (2)*.
Use the clock face in **Question 6** to help you.

8 a) There are ☐ seconds in 1 minute.

b) There are ☐ minutes in 1 hour.

c) There are ☐ hours in 1 day.

9 Fill in **a.m.** or **p.m.**

a) It is 3.00 __.__.

b) It is 3.00 __.__.

c) Midnight to noon is __.__.   d) Noon to midnight is __.__.

e) Morning is __.__.   f) Night-time is __.__.

g) Afternoon is __.__.   h) Evening is __.__.

24-hour clock

We can show **a.m.** or **p.m.** in another way.
The clock could look like this to show the **24 hours** in a day.

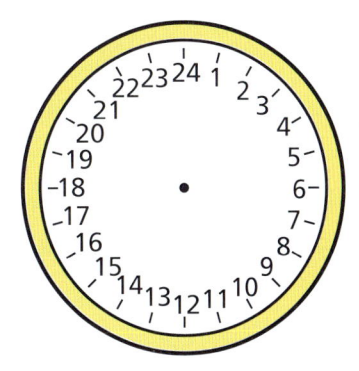

Instead, the small (hour) hand has to make
two journeys around the clock in **1 day**.

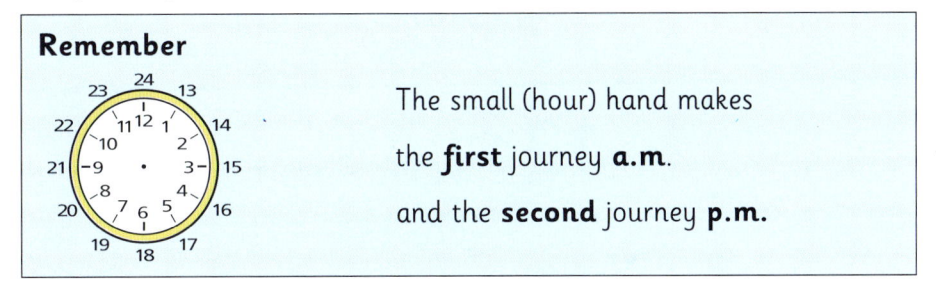

> **Remember**
>
> The small (hour) hand makes
> the **first** journey **a.m.**
> and the **second** journey **p.m.**

We write the 24-hour times with four digits – like this.

01:00 is 1 o'clock **a.m.**   01:15 is 1.15 **a.m.**
13:00 is 1 o'clock **p.m.**   13:15 is 1.15 **p.m.**

10 Write the **24-hour clock times** for these **p.m. times**.
The two dots : separate the hours from the minutes.

a) 2.00 p.m. = 14:00

b) 4.00 p.m.   c) 8.00 p.m.   d) 1.00 p.m.   e) 10.00 p.m.

f) 6.00 p.m.   g) 7.00 p.m.   h) 11.00 p.m.   i) 5.00 p.m.

186 UNIT 12 MEASURES

11 Write the **p.m. times** for these **24-hour clock times**.
The two dots : separate the hours from the minutes.

a) 14:00 = 2.00 p.m.

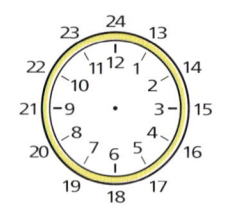

b) 22:00   c) 19:00   d) 21:00   e) 18:00

f) 20:00   g) 13:00   h) 17:00   i) 15:00

12 Try Worksheet 4 *24-hour clock*.

13 Copy **only** the **p.m.** times.

a) 01:30   13:30   1.30 afternoon   1.30 morning

a) 13:30   1.30 afternoon

b) 15:20   3.20 afternoon   3.20 morning   03:20

c) 7.15 evening   7.15 morning   19:15   07:15

d) 4.10 morning   04:10   16:10   4.10 afternoon

Time: 24-hour clock and calendars 187

14 Try Worksheet 5 *My day*.

15 Tom's family are going to a football match in London.

FA Cup Final
Leeds v Liverpool
Wembley Stadium
3.00pm 18th April

They catch a train which leaves at **quarter past 12**.

The timetable looks like this.

Depart York	Arrive King's Cross London
11:15	13:15
12:15	14:15
13:15	15:15
14:15	16:15
15:15	17:15
16:15	18:15

a) The time their train departs is written as _____.

b) The time their train arrives is written as _____.

c) The journey will take ☐ hours.

d) Copy the timetable and fill in the times as 12-hour clock times.

> **Remember**
>
> Write **a.m.** or **p.m.**

e) Fill in with **early** or **late**.

The family arrived _____ at the station.

f) It takes about an hour to get from the station to the match.
Do you think Tom's family left enough time?
What train would you have taken to London?
Which of these trains do you think they could take back to York?

Depart King's Cross London	Arrive York
16:30	18:30
17:30	19:30
18:30	20:30
19:30	21:30
20:30	22:30
21:30	23:30

Calendars

16 Tom wrote the date of the big match on his calendar. Look at the other things he wrote.

	APRIL					
Sun	Mon	Tue	Wed	Thurs	Fri	Sat
			1	2	Break up ③ Easter	④ Disco
5	6	My ⑦ birthday	8	9	10	11
12	13	14	15	16	17	Match in ⑱ London
19	Back to ⑳ school	21	22	23	24	25
26	27	28	29	10 o'clock ㉚ Dentist		

a) The match was on a _____ .

b) Tom's birthday was on the first _____ of the month.

c) The visit to the dentist was on a _____ .

d) The disco was on a _____ .

e) The Easter holidays were ☐ weeks long.

f) There were ☐ days between Tom's birthday and the match.

g) Tom went back to school ☐ days after the match.

h) The disco was ☐ days before Tom's birthday.

i) Explain why there are blank squares in the calendar above.

UNIT 12 MEASURES

17 Try Worksheet 6 *Short dates*.

18 Write the dates of all the Fridays in the calendar month shown in **Question 16**.

> **Remember**
> We write dates like this:
> Friday 3rd April 1998

19 Try Worksheets 7 and 8 *Calendar planner (1), (2)*.

20 Copy the present calendar month.
Fill in reminders for yourself.

21 Look at these dates.
For **each** date write down the dates of:

- the next day
- the day before

- a week earlier
- a week later

- a month earlier
- a month later

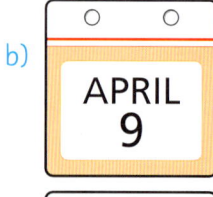

a) MAY 14

b) APRIL 9

c) MARCH 16

d) JUNE 20

Time: 24-hour clock and calendars 191

22 Sue was born on 23rd August 1991.

Lee was born on 23rd November 1991.

Ali was born on 2nd July 1990.

Ben was born on 21st May 1993.

a) Who is the **oldest**?

b) Who is the **youngest**?
To find the answer, talk about which you should look at **first**: the **date**, the **month** or the **year**.

23 a) Put in order – **earliest time** first.

2.30 a.m.   16:15   4.15 a.m.   18:45

$\frac{1}{2}$ past 2 in the afternoon

b) Put in order – **shortest period of time** first.

| month | minute | day | hour |
| second | year | week | |

24 Try Worksheet Puzzle *TV Times*.

25 You need
- Unit 12 Race against time cards
- your 'My maths record' sheet.

Race against time

1 Sort the race cards – this side up

> 16:45

2 Take the cards one at a time.

3 Answer as quickly as you can:
'Quarter to five p.m.'

4 Did you get it right?
Look at the other side of the card.

> $\frac{1}{4}$ to 5 p.m.

5 When you get all the answers correct, ask a friend to test you.

6 Now **Race against time**.

Go for points!

Ask your teacher to test and time you.

> **Remember**
>
> 3 errors – 1 point
>
> 2 errors – 2 points
>
> 1 error – 3 points
>
> 0 errors – 5 points
>
> Answer in 1 minute with 0 errors – 7 points

Now try Unit 12 Test.

Time: 24-hour clock and calendars 193

Review 12

1 Find the bill for each of these meals.

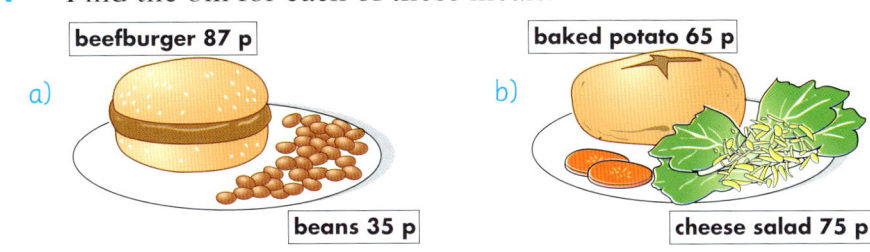

a) beefburger 87 p
beans 35 p

b) baked potato 65 p
cheese salad 75 p

2 Joe saves £84. How much has he left each time if he spends:

a) £40?   b) £4?   c) £14?

d) £26?   e) £9?   f) £38?

3 Write in order – **smallest** number first.

456   1241   406   46   1421   64

4 To help me remember, my:

a) **30 cm reminder** is _____

b) **1 m reminder** is _____

c) **1 kg reminder** is _____

d) **1 l reminder** is _____

UNIT 12 MEASURES

5
a) $4 \times 2 = \square$
b) $2 \times \square = 8$
c) $4 \times \square = 8$
d) $8 \div 2 = \square$
e) $8 \div \square = 2$
f) $8 \div \square = 4$

6 Write down the number **before** and the number **after** these numbers.

a) $\square$ 279 $\square$
b) $\square$ 199 $\square$
c) $\square$ 400 $\square$
d) $\square$ 999 $\square$

7 Write these amounts – use the £ sign and a **decimal point**.

a) 184p
b) 193p
c) 328p
d) 812p
e) 548p
f) 350p

8 Which scale?

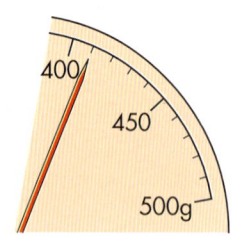

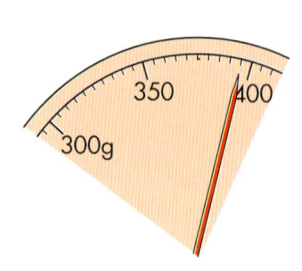

a) The marks are going up in $\square$. The weight is $\square$ g.
b) The marks are going up in $\square$. The weight is $\square$ g